Chasing God, Manifesting Your Dreams

Felicia R. Phillips, MDiv

Chasing God, Manifesting Your Dreams

Copyright © 2017 by Felicia R. Phillips, MDiv

FeliciaRPhillips.com

Published by Through His Eyes Publishing
Morton, PA

All Rights Reserved. No part of this publication may be reproduced, stored in a retrieval system, or transmitted in any form or by any means – electronic, mechanical, photocopy, recording, or any other – except for brief quotations in printed reviews, without the prior permission of the publisher.

Scriptures are taken from the Holy Bible King James Version unless otherwise noted.

ISBN 978-0-99938833-0-8

Printed in the United States of America

November 2017

Editor: Stephanie Montgomery
Cover Photo: Leaping Lion Photography
Cover Art: Janet Dado

Acknowledgements

Words cannot express the gratitude I have for the special individuals God sent during various stages of my journey in completing my first book project. I should probably do this in some sort of order that makes sense; and while my order makes sense to me, it may not to you. Just work with me.

I want to first and foremost give honor to my Lord and Savior Jesus Christ. I am so blessed to have accepted Jesus Christ at the age of 8 years old. Since then, the hand of God and His anointing have been all over my life. Although I did not always realize it, I know now that God created me with a purpose and a plan. Over my many blessed years on this earth, God has molded and shaped me into the woman of God He created me to be. He has poured so much into me, including gifts and talents beyond measure. He laid the path for me to walk into my destiny.

I thank God for His undying, unwavering and unconditional love for me. I thank God for His grace and mercy. I thank God for sending His only begotten Son into this world to save a wretch like me. He did not have to do it and I did not deserve it - yet, He loved me so much that He was willing to make the sacrifice. For that, I give Him praise. I thank Him for the vision. I thank Him for seeing me as a minister of the Gospel, long before I ever saw myself as a minister. I thank Him for seeing me as an international speaker and preacher. I thank Him for seeing me as a published author. I thank Him for opening my spiritual eyes so that I could see myself the way He has always seen me. I truly believe I am what God sees. I am a published author and I thank and give glory to God for allowing me to write and publish this book.

Next, I want to acknowledge two very special people. While they were not directly involved in the book project, I owe all that I am today to their faithfulness in raising me to love God with all of my heart; for initiating my appreciation of sound biblical teaching from Sunday School through seminary and for laying the foundation of everything I do for Jesus Christ. Thank you Mommy and Daddy, Beverly and John Bey - for loving me, caring for me, protecting me, providing for me and supporting me. This book is the fruit of the excellent job you did as parents. I pray that you are proud of your baby girl!

Whenever God gives you a major assignment, Satan will surely show up and try to show out - but how many know that with God, you are a majority? How many know that when two or three are gathered together in His name, God is in the midst? How many know that the effectual, fervent prayers of the righteous availeth much? How many know that prayer works? I am a living testimony, because I have had many people praying for me over the past few years – however three specific ladies interceded on my behalf excessively: Rev. Shani Johnson, Rev. Jamie Eaddy and Dr. Sarah Langley. What a blessing it was to be vulnerable and transparent with these women during my darkest hours and to know that they were praying me through. I praise God for each of you and pray that God will pour into your lives as you have poured so much into mine.

Acknowledgements

And I have to give a special shout out to Dr. Sarah Langley for allowing God to use her to help me dream big and believe God for more. I have to give credit where credit is due. I praise God for using you to push me.

I praise God for using you to challenge me. I praise God for using you to help me see myself the way God really saw me and for urging me to walk in my divine calling. Thank you and God bless you as you travel the world and continue to empower, inspire and motivate women to live their very best lives without regret.

And what about my innermost circle – the crew that gets the good, the bad and the ugly side many never have the opportunity to see? The crew that God placed in my life to listen to my worries, concerns and fears, offer advice, share, love and support plain old Felicia Renee Phillips. Not Minister Felicia Phillips. Not the preacher. Not the teacher. Not the marketing communications strategist. Not the international speaker. Just me in all of my beauty and ugliness. These ladies are my cheerleaders, prayer partners, counselors and so much more. They listened to various ideas, looked at design concept after design concept, endured a million text messages and kept me motivated from start to finish. I bless God for you Alesia Mitchell Bailey and Danielle Gadson. This book would not have made it past my iPad without your support and prayers.

I also want to thank others I know who are always praying for me: Shukura Monroe - a friend for over 25 years, Tanesha Samples - who is known to go 'ham for the lamb' and Minister Dawn Duppins - who always has a kind, motivating word. I also want to thank a dear friend and prayer warrior, Marlita Thompson; she is so in tune to the Spirit of God - I know my name is called in prayer at just the right time. I would be remiss if I did not thank Dr. Yashima White AziLove - one of my very first coaches and a paragon of virtue and strength. You encouraged me to look for God's exceeding abundance in every aspect of my life; work, family and ministry and to expect God's blessing to overtake me as I claim my inheritance as a child of the King.

I thank Pastor Monica Haskell (or PM as we affectionately call her), an amazing woman of God and entrepreneur who lit the fire inside of me and pushed me to write this book. Before I met you less than a year ago, writing a book was merely a dream - however when I connected with you, I connected with destiny. It was a divine appointment. To be honest, I was afraid to get too close at first because I did not want you exposing my excuses. However, I gradually opened myself to your divine purpose in my life and because of your tutelage, I now have manifestation in the form of this book. God bless you Pastor Monica Haskell.

In memoriam, I must acknowledge Deacon William Chaplain Denise Dinkins. Both of these special individuals (who in my faulty opinion are gone too soon), played important roles in helping me grow spiritually, seek the face of God, trust His plans and stand firm on His Word. Deacon Eubanks was my mentor and teacher extraordinaire. He saw something in me many years ago I did not quite see. He saw a glimpse of where God was taking me and he accepted his assignment to guide me through a portion of my journey. I am forever grateful for his instruction, wisdom, sound biblical teaching and prayers. I am also grateful for his obedience to share what the Lord gave him to speak to me no matter what. He is one of the primary reasons I finally started seminary in 2006 and his guidance helped me push through to graduation and beyond.

Acknowledgements

And what can I say about Chaplain Dinkins? I did not realize until after her death, that she was such an instrumental part of my life. She was a blessing from the moment we first met. She was a teacher, role model, mentor, prayer warrior, prayer intercessor, preacher and lover of God. Not only did Chaplain Dinkins teach me the Word of God - she taught me the importance of BELIEVING the Word of God. She was a woman of enormous faith who was unafraid to testify to the goodness of God. As I discerned my call into ministry, she was right there encouraging me throughout the entire process.

To my special girls, Kyra and Kaitlyn; I want to say that I love you and thank God for blessing me with both of you. While finishing this book was major to me, you both responded to this accomplishment the same way you responded to so many others previously - as if it's nothing special. I used to be bothered by that until I realized that I raised both of you to aspire to greatness and that you expect no less of me. You expect me to achieve. You expect me to walk in my destiny. You expect favor to cover my life. You expect me to do great things that bring God glory.

I thank and praise God for you Kyra and Kaitlyn, for the sacrifices you've made - not only as I embarked upon this book project, but throughout your entire lives as I sought to answer God's call. My goal was always to be the best mother I could while walking in my purpose, teaching you about God's amazing love and being an example of a woman of God living a life which brings God glory. My prayer is that you will continue to follow my lead in chasing after God and manifesting the dreams He has placed inside of you.

And finally, to the man God blessed me with so many years ago - I start with a huge thank you. I praise God for you

Felicia R. Phillips

Robert Thomas Phillips. You have been my biggest supporter and cheerleader. You have seen the ugly that even my inner circle has not seen and you still loved me through. You remained by my side through thick and thin. You have pushed me, stretched me, challenged me, encouraged me and held me accountable to my goals. You have been a cook, house cleaner, chauffeur, counselor and so much more. You have been my prayer partner and spiritual protector. This book would not have been possible without you. I love you so much and I praise God for blessing me with such a wonderful man of God. You are everything I need in a help-mate and more. God made no mistakes when He joined us together.

     I decided to write this book during a challenging time in our lives. With so much going on, it seemed as if I would never finish - but you took on extra tasks around the house and with our girls to give me the space to do what was needed. You believed in me and believed in my dreams even when I often doubted they would come to pass. Your love and support make dreaming easy. Your prayers keep me in line as we chase God together. I love you with all of my heart and I dedicate this book to you and our forever love.

Table of Contents

Acknowledgements 3

Introduction 11

Chapter 1: *Chasing and Dreaming* 15

Chapter 2: *Lessons from Joseph* 27

Chapter 3: *God Chasers Have Power* 37

Chapter 4: *Be Strong and Courageous* 47

Chapter 5: *On the Run* 57

Chapter 6: *Dream Haters* 65

Chapter 7: *Dream Big* 73

Chapter 8: *Check Your Circle* 79

Chapter 9: *Take the First Step* 87

Chapter 10: *See Yourself Through God's Eyes* 95

Chapter 11: *Don't Quit* 101

Conclusion 109

Introduction

We often hear that success is not a destination, but rather a journey. I would venture to say the same of chasing God and manifesting your dreams. As long as you are on this earth, I encourage you to pursue God with your entire being. Chase after Him and the dreams He has given you and when you realize one dream - seek God more, as you will soon discover God has placed multiple dreams inside of you. What is even better is that God is able to bring every single dream to pass.

Before I go any further, I want to thank you for purchasing my debut book; Chasing God, Manifesting Your Dreams. Writing a book was just one of the many dreams I always had for my life. I know it was a dream that only God placed in my heart and one that only God was able to bring to pass. The fact that you are reading it means the world to me. My prayer is that you will be blessed by what you read as you draw closer to God, uncover the dreams He has for your life and move toward manifestation.

I am so very excited that you have entrusted me to participate in this journey with you. I hope that you are equally excited. At the same time, I am sure you are also a little curious about what this journey entails, so let me explain. As you read this book, you are going to learn two things. First, you will learn what it means to be a God chaser. Second, you will learn how God chasers manifest their dreams.

Now, in order to get the most out of this book, I do want to point out one assumption I already made about you as the reader; I am assuming that you are a Believer. In other words, I assume that you have accepted Jesus Christ as your personal Lord and Savior in accordance with Romans 10:9 *"That if thou shalt confess with thy mouth the Lord Jesus, and shalt believe in thine heart that God hath raised him from the dead, thou shalt be saved. For with the heart man believeth unto righteousness; and with the mouth confession is made unto salvation."*

Hopefully, you are still reading and hopefully you are a Christian. However, if I have made an erroneous assumption - I apologize. But I also want to offer an invitation for you to accept Jesus Christ as your personal Lord and Savior and to join the body of Believers across the world. As the scripture states, it is as simple as confessing and believing. If you confess that Jesus Christ is the Son of the Living God, sent into the world to die for your sins and believe in your heart that God raised Jesus from the dead - you can receive the free gift of salvation.

This short prayer sums it up and makes it easy for you to make Jesus the Lord of your life. All you have to do is repeat the prayer and believe:

Dear Lord,

I confess that I am a sinner. I believe that Jesus Christ died on the cross to save me from sins. I believe that on the third day, Jesus rose from the grave with all power in His hands. Thank you Lord for saving me. In Jesus' name. Amen.

Introduction

Welcome to the body of Christ. Now, in addition to reading this book, I am praying that you will find a Christ-centered, Bible-based, Spirit-filled church where you can learn, grow and serve in the kingdom of God. If you need help finding a church home, email me at frpministries@hotmail.com and I will be happy to assist you.

Your relationship with God will help you to better understand the content of this book, whether you are a newly-saved individual or a more seasoned saint. So, how does it work? I am glad you asked. The first half of this book will focus on what it means to be a God chaser and why it is important to chase God before you manifest your dreams. In the second half of the book, I will share vital tips for God chasers to manifest their dreams.

Please approach this book with an open heart ready to hear and receive from the Lord as you chase after God and manifest your dreams. Are you ready God chasers? I certainly know that I am! But before you turn the page, I want to mention one more thing. Each chapter of the book ends with a prayer that is related to the chapter. Not only do I want to share key information about chasing God and manifesting your dreams - I also want to seal it with a Word of prayer, just like this:

Dear Lord,

I thank you for every individual reading this book. I pray that you will bless them as they start or continue their journey of chasing after you and manifesting the dreams you have placed inside of them.

Lord, I do not know every single person's story, but I do know you. I know that you love all of your children. I know that you sent your

Son, Jesus the Christ, to die on the cross at Calvary in order to save us from our sins. I know that we are redeemed by the precious blood of Jesus.

Lord, I thank you for the purpose and the plan you have for each one of your children. I thank you for the dreams you have planted in our hearts as seeds which will only grow as we seek your face through prayer, studying your Word and serving in your kingdom.

Often we try to do things in our own strength, but right now, I ask that you would give us the holy boldness and faith to relinquish ourselves to you. Help us to seek you for wisdom, understanding, direction, resources, divine connections and appointments. Let your favor accompany us wherever we go.

And as we chase after you, I thank you that you will manifest every dream that you have given us. Manifest the hidden dreams Lord. Manifest the forgotten dreams Lord. Manifest the abandoned dreams. We can't do it by ourselves - but with you, all things are possible.

Thank you in advance for choosing us to do great things. Thank you for choosing us to manifest big dreams. We declare with our mouths today that we are God chasers and we will manifest our God-given dreams. In Jesus' Name, Amen.

CHAPTER 1
Chasing and Dreaming

While the title of this chapter is *Chasing and Dreaming*, I'd actually like to start with dreaming, mix in a little chasing and then return to dreaming. Let's get started. What is a dream? Merriam Webster's Online Dictionary lists several definitions for the word dream, but for our purposes I would like to focus on just two definitions. According to Merriam-Webster.com; a dream can be defined as 'a series of thoughts, images, or emotions occurring during sleep' or 'a strongly desired goal or purpose.' While the majority of this book will focus on the second definition, I wanted to acknowledge the first definition and here is why: God sometimes places a dream (a strongly desired goal or purpose) in your heart and He will reveal it in a dream (a series of thoughts, images or emotions occurring during sleep).

During my freshman year in college, I had a dream where I saw myself preaching. I was already saved, born again and raised in the church, however preaching was the farthest thing from my mind. Although I was beginning to voluntarily chase after God, I was also very young and looking to fit in and enjoy my experience at the HBCU (Historically Black College and University for those unfamiliar with the term) I was attending. I knew enough to share the dream with my pastor, but after that, I pretty much moved on with my life. I was thinking, 'I'd like to see how you make that happen God'. That is exactly what He did.

God planted the seed in my heart to preach the Gospel through a dream that happened 20 years before preaching became my dream! My God. If we were in church, I would be shouting right now. This is clearly a "Won't He do it?" moment. But I digress. Not only did God plant the preaching seed in my heart, thereby giving me a glimpse of my future through a dream; He also began to water that seed as I slowly began chasing after Him. As I chased after God during my collegiate years, my relationship with God and my prayer life really began to flourish.

By the time I graduated from college, I had really started seeking God's purpose for my life and my greatest desire was to please Him. My whole view on life changed. I was no longer living my life and doing things based on what I wanted; instead, I constantly sought direction from God, waiting for Him to reveal His will. I asked God to order my steps. I wanted to be used by God. I wanted to bring glory to His name. And so, I began to seek God's face. I wanted to know Him more and more. I spent time in worship, while God watered the seed. I spent time in Bible study, while God watered the seed. I spent time in prayer, while God watered the seed.

In 2000, I started attending biblical classes at the Mt. Airy Religious Training Institute (MARTI), a biblical school at my home church during that time - Mt. Airy Church of God in Christ in Philadelphia, PA. I took classes on the Old Testament, New Testament, Cult and World Religions, the Revelation and even a class on Spiritual Warfare. In fact, the year I took the spiritual warfare class was the same year I heard the voice of God calling me into ministry. Reflecting on that dream in college when I saw myself preaching, I said yes to the call.

But let's not end the story there. In 2006, I enrolled as a student of the Urban Theological Institute at the Lutheran Theological Institute in Philadelphia to get my Master of Divinity. As part of my studies, I was required to do an internship at a local church. I opted to return to the church of my youth - Miller Memorial Baptist Church (MMBC). During my time at MMBC, I had the privilege of preaching a service for youth.

I preached a message based on Genesis 50:20 entitled, 'But God had a Plan.' The message was about the dream God placed in Joseph's heart as a child and all that transpired in Joseph's life between the time God gave Joseph the dream until it came to pass. We will talk about that story in greater detail later in the book. Studying and meditating on God's word in preparation for preaching that message reminded me of the dream God placed in my own heart as a young college student and everything I experienced between then until I attended seminary to prepare myself for ordained ministry. Will you look at God? Through that experience, I learned how to chase God and manifest dreams.

But enough about me; at least for now. I have two questions for you. First, are you a God chaser? Before you answer, let me share more about what that actually means. My oldest daughter, Kyra used to lead a song in the choir called "Chasing After You" by Vashawn Mitchell. While the lyrics of the song paint a nice picture of what it means to be a God chaser - so does the Word of God. To be crystal clear, a God chaser is like the psalmist in Psalm 42:1 who proclaimed, *"As the hart panteth after the water brooks, so panteth my soul after thee, O God."* A God chaser thirsts for more of God. A God chaser is like the psalmist in Psalm 16:1, who declared, "*Thou wilt shew me the path of life: in thy presence is fullness of joy; at thy right hand there are pleasures for evermore.*" A God chaser wants more of God's presence. A God chaser is just like the psalmist in Psalm 63:1, who exclaims, "*O God, thou art my God; early will I seek thee: my soul thirsteth for thee…*" A God chaser does not mind getting up early to be in the presence of God.

A God chaser follows the very same counsel God gave Joshua after the death of Moses – "*This book of the law shall not depart out of thy mouth; but thou shalt meditate therein day and night, that thou mayest observe to do according to all that is written therein: for then thou shalt make thy way prosperous, and then thou shalt have good success*" (Joshua 1:8). A God chaser doesn't just read the Word of God: a God chaser studies and meditates on the Word of God day and night. A God chaser doesn't just hear the Word: a God chaser obeys the Word. A God chaser is not only found worshipping God on Sunday - a God chaser worships God every single day of the week. A God chaser seeks counsel from God. A God chaser remains still and listens to the voice of the Lord. Lastly, a God chaser manifests dreams - which leads to my second series of questions.

Are you a dreamer? Do you wake up with memories about the dreams you had overnight? Can you recall your dreams in great detail or do you only recall fragments of your dreams, if anything at all?

You already know at least one of my dreams and how God spoke to me about preaching. But God does not always speak to me when I dream. Sometimes my dreams don't mean anything. They are merely residue from my previous day's activities or whatever I read or watched before going to bed. I might fall asleep after watching an episode of a favorite crime show where a young, beautiful woman is abducted by a bad guy in a typical white van;

then suddenly I find myself transported to a scene in my dream where I am the young, beautiful woman being kidnapped! I am sure this happens to many people, maybe even you.

While those types of dreams don't typically carry any significant meaning - there are other times (like when God allowed me to see myself preaching), when my dreams are much more meaningful. Those are the dreams that I know come from God. God allows me to have those dreams for a reason because they carry tremendous significance. God speaks to me through those types of dreams. God shares His vision for my life through those types of dreams. God reveals purpose through those types of dreams. God even warns, corrects or rebukes me in those types of dreams.

Here is an example of a warning God gave me in a dream. In the winter of 1999, I was living with my boyfriend, who is now my husband. He proposed to me over the Christmas holiday and of course, I said yes. We were both saved and Spirit-filled, but not in fellowship with a local church. One day, I dreamed that I was dressed in a full wedding gown and veil, but I was in a cemetery. In the dream, I saw a burial plot that was already prepared and a coffin. I also saw myself fully clothed in the wedding attire, step down into the casket and lie down.

When I awakened from that dream, I thought it was the craziest thing. Soon after, I remember catching up with an old friend from my high school gospel choir over the phone. We were having a casual conversation, then I shared my crazy dream with him. To my surprise, God immediately gave him an interpretation. My friend said almost verbatim, "I don't know where you and your boyfriend are spiritually right now, but if you stay in this place and get married, it will result in your spiritual death."

I was in complete shock that God spoke through my dream and enabled me to speak with a friend who would give a spot-on interpretation of the dream! My husband had just moved to Philadelphia from Atlanta and hadn't met my friends yet, so only the Holy Spirit could have revealed this interpretation. Remember I mentioned we were both out of fellowship? My husband stopped going to the church we both attended in Atlanta while I was in college and although I moved back to Philadelphia the previous year, I hadn't settled in a church home.

God warned us through my dream that our relationship with Him and with each other was headed in the wrong direction. Of course we repented and immediately began searching for a church home. We returned to Mt. Airy Church of God in Christ - the church I attended right before going to college. On December 31, 1999, we both decided to join the church and get our spiritual house in order, which is exactly what we did.

You may not relate to my experience with dreams. In fact, you may not even consider yourself a dreamer. You may not believe that you dream every night or even at all. But guess what? Dreaming is not just something I do - it is something that you do as well. We are all dreamers. We all dream every single night. Now God may not always speak to you through your dreams as He does with me; we have our own unique relationship with God and He speaks to us differently, however you are dreaming whether God speaks or not.

I can hear some of you right now saying, "I never have dreams." This simply is not true, nor is it supported by science. According to www.sleep.org - a website powered by the National Sleep Foundation; "You generally dream at least 4 to 6 times per night, usually during the most active REM stage of sleep". Think about that for a moment. Think about how many times you actually dream. An average of four to six dreams per night, equates to approximately 28 dreams per week. This is roughly 112 dreams per month and 1344 dreams per year! Now that is a lot of dreaming.

By now you're probably wondering what is the point of all this talk about dreaming? Well, I assume that if you are reading this book, then you are or desire to become a God chaser who manifests dreams. We have examined what it means to be a God chaser, so let's explore what it takes in order to manifest your dreams. In order to chase after God and manifest your dreams, you must be more than just a dreamer; you must be a bold dreamer who takes action and you must believe that your dreams can come true. Note that I had the dream about preaching, but then went to seminary. I had a dream just like the other 7.5 billion people in the world, but then I was bold enough to take action – and now my dream has manifested!

Dreamers live in 'la-la land,' where they dream constantly without any manifestation. Bold dreamers understand that their dreams will remain only dreams if they stay in the same place. Bold dreamers make things happen. Bold dreamers push past challenges. Bold dreamers fight against obstacles. Bold dreamers believe in themselves and their dreams - no matter how small or great. Bold dreamers manifest their dreams!

Let's consider a few other bold dreamers. How about author, executive producer, actress, talk show host, network owner and business mogul Oprah Winfrey? Anyone familiar with Oprah's story is aware she dreamed of one day being in front of the camera, just like so many other dreamers enrolled in journalism programs. One day, Oprah got her big break; she was offered a highly-coveted anchor role at a television station in Baltimore, Maryland. Long before she hosted the Oprah Winfrey Show - which aired for an amazing 25 years however, the now billionaire was fired from her first on-camera role at that news station and told she was not good enough.

What about Gabrielle Douglas? This little girl from Newport News, Virginia had a dream - remember, everyone does. Gabby was a bold dreamer. She believed in herself and in her ability to make her dreams come true and she took action! Going to the Olympics was a huge dream for the child of a single mom struggling to raise three children, but that was Gabby's dream and it did not end there. Gabby dreamed of going to the Olympics and winning - and she did! Gabby was the first African American in Olympic history to become the individual all-around champion and first U.S. gymnast to win gold in the individual and team competitions at the 2012 Olympics. She brought home a gold medal as part of the Final Five in Team Competition during the 2016 Olympics as well.

Does anyone know Simone Manuel? In the not-so-distant past, swimming pools were segregated. Black people were not allowed to swim in the same pools as white people. In 2016, a 20-year old Black girl with a dream, swam in the Olympics among the best swimmers in the world. This bold dreamer became the first African-American woman to win an individual gold medal in swimming and set both Olympic and American records. She is just one of several determined dreamers we could mention, like Steve Jobs, Tyler Perry, Serena Williams, Arianna Huffington, Lisa Nichols and even President Barack Obama!

I hope these examples help you understand there is nothing special about dreaming in and of itself. Everybody dreams. Dreaming is normal. Dreaming is typical. Dreaming is common. Dreaming is usual. Dreaming is ordinary. Some people specialize in dreaming and do nothing more than dream. Then there are bold dreamers; those individuals who have a dream, believe it can come to pass, then take action. If you want to see dreams manifest, you must do more than just dream - you have to boldly pursue it. That is the reason for this book.

It is my sincere hope and prayer that by the end of this book, you will be equipped with biblical principles to pursue your God-given dreams with confidence, take the limits off and walk into your destiny. Before we delve into that, I want to spend a moment expanding on a thought I mentioned earlier. While God does place dreams in our hearts, it is critical to understand that every dream is not from God. This is so important I want to say it again; every dream we have is not from God.

At times, we get caught chasing everyone's dream except God's dream. Instead of boldly pursuing dreams God gives us - we chase our own dreams or even the dreams of others, then we pretend that the dreams we struggle to manifest actually came from God. Perhaps your mother always dreamed you would grow up to become a doctor like her, but God is saying He wants to use you in foreign missions. Whose dream do you chase? Maybe your father wants you to become a pastor just like him and his father, but God wants you to educate and mentor inner city children. Whose dream do you chase? Perhaps your mentor is trying to encourage you to start your own business, but God is telling you to plant a new church. Whose dream do you chase? Maybe your supervisor wants to promote you to a new position, but God wants you to remain where you are to minister to your co-workers. Whose dream do you chase? Maybe you want to stay in the same position at the company where you've been for the past 10 years, but God wants to stretch you in a new position at a new company. Whose dream do you chase? God chasers chase God and manifest the dreams God gives them.

Often we chase things like money, fame, power and status instead of chasing God. We make acquiring things more important than deepening our relationship with God through His Son Jesus Christ. God can give us any and everything - however, He does so in His timing and in accordance with His will. Consider this: God promises us in Matthew 6:33, *"But seek ye first the kingdom of God, and his righteousness; and all these things shall be added unto you."* Seeking God first means chasing after Him - not things. If we seek God's kingdom and His righteousness, then the dreams He placed inside of us will come to pass. We will experience the blessings that come from a right relationship with God and our God-given dreams will be manifested.

Do you remember how God placed the goal of being a preacher in my heart? If you recall, I did not take any action at first. As I began chasing after God however, God's dream became my dream - then I began my bold pursuit. In doing so, I was chasing God's dream, purpose and plan for my life. And guess what? When God places a dream in our heart and we chase after Him, that God-given dream will come to pass.

Unfortunately, far too many are not manifesting dreams: this is because they are not from God. There is a difference - as I've explained, between pursuing ours and everyone else's dreams and chasing God's dreams. God's dreams for us are tied into our destiny. God's dreams are tied into the unique purpose and plan He has for our advancement into the kingdom of God, bringing glory to His name. The reasons some of your dreams have failed is because you were not chasing God-given dreams. But that is about to change right now - believe it and receive it. Chase God and manifest your dreams!

Dear Lord,

I thank you for allowing me to read this book on chasing God and manifesting dreams. Help me to truly understand what it means to be a God chaser. Help me to seek your face and to develop a more intimate relationship with you. Help me to discern your voice. Help me to know the difference between chasing after the dreams of someone else and chasing after the dreams that you have placed in my heart. I want to be a God chaser and I want to manifest the dreams that you have for my life. I surrender to you and believe that it will come to pass. In Jesus' name I pray. Amen.

CHAPTER 2
Lessons from Joseph

The story of Joseph, found in the book of Genesis, provides us with an incredible example of what it means to chase God and literally manifest your dreams. The story ends in Egypt with the reassuring words of Joseph speaking to his older brothers, as found in Genesis 50:20 - *"But as for you, ye thought evil against me; but God meant it unto good, to bring to pass, as it is this day, to save much people alive."* However, Joseph's story begins much earlier in the book of Genesis.

For the purpose of our focus on dreams, we will start in Genesis 37 where we find 17-year old Joseph, the son of Jacob and Rachel and the great-grandson of Abraham the patriarch. Joseph is a young man who was loved dearly by his father, yet despised by his older brothers. Genesis 37:3-4 sheds some light on why Joseph's brothers hated him; *"Now Israel loved Joseph more than all his children, because he was the son of his old age: and he made him a coat of many colours. And when his brethren saw that their father loved him more than all his brethren, they hated him, and could not speak peaceably unto him."*

These verses reveal that Jacob loved his son Joseph more than his other children. The scripture also reveals that Jacob loved

Joseph's mother Rachel, far more than other his wife Leah. Genesis 29:30, *"And he went in also unto Rachel, and he loved also Rachel more than Leah, and served with him yet seven other years."* Therefore, it makes sense that Jacob favored the first born of his favorite wife.

Jacob's other children knew that Joseph was the favored child. Adding insult to injury, Jacob did not try to hide the favoritism. Let's review Genesis 37:4 again; it says, *"And when his brothers saw that their father loved him more than all his brethren, they hated him and could not speak peaceably to him."* Have you ever had someone - maybe a neighbor, classmate, coworker, or even a close relative who could not stand you because of the favor on your life? Well, this is what occurred with Joseph, the favorite son of Jacob.

In the words of some of my younger readers, you might say Joseph's brothers were 'hating'. They hated their younger brother and never had a kind word to share with him, especially when Joseph told them about his dreams. Joseph shared his first dream with his brothers in Genesis 37:7, *"We were out in the field, tying up bundles of grain. Suddenly my bundle stood up, and your bundles all gathered around and bowed low before mine!"* In the second dream, which he shared with his brothers in verse 9; *"…the sun, moon and eleven stars bowed low before him!"*

I can only imagine the response of Joseph's brothers. Think about it; Joseph is the second youngest child of Jacob and also the favorite. He basically tells his brothers he dreamed that he was going to rise above them and that they would bow down to him. That is like walking up to someone who doesn't like you at work, church or perhaps a professional organization and telling them you dreamed you were going to be their boss. I can hear the response so clearly right now; "Bye Felicia!"

Joseph's brothers hated Joseph even more after he shared his dream, which is why you must truly chase God in order to manifest your dreams. Chasing God will allow you to discern when you should share your dreams and with whom. Unfortunately, not everyone is happy about the fact that you have a dream. Those are the individuals who lack enthusiasm when you share your dreams. Those are individuals who brush off your big dreams. Those are the individuals who laugh or mock your dreams. Those are the individuals, who like Joseph's brothers - we refer to as haters.

Haters will shoot down your dreams because they don't have the courage to dream big. Haters will shoot down your dreams, because they don't believe their own dreams will come true. Haters will shoot down your dreams because they are afraid your dreams will actually come to fruition. Haters will shoot down your dreams because they are not bold enough to pursue their own. Haters will tell you they can't see you going to college, moving out of the hood, getting married, finding a job, launching a business or preaching the Gospel. But God chasers stand on the Word of God in Philippians 4:13, *"I can do all things through Christ which strengthenth me."*

If God gave you a dream, keep chasing God until it comes to pass. If God has spoken a Word into your life, believe God and chase after Him until it manifests. It may be tempting to listen to what haters say, but remember the word of God in Proverbs 18:21, *"Death and life are in the power of the tongue: and they that love it shall eat the fruit thereof."* Do not let haters kill your dreams with their words. I offer a different response for God chasers.

God chasers know exactly how to respond to haters. That is why it is so important to chase God in order to manifest your dreams. Haters always have lots to say. Haters will talk and spew out lies that do not align with your God-given dreams. Meanwhile,

God chasers are already prepared with a response. God chasers are armed and equipped with the Word of God.

Remember when Jesus was tempted by Satan in the wilderness? How did Jesus respond to Satan? Jesus, our chief God chaser, responded with the Word of God. Look at Matthew 4:11, *"Then was Jesus led up of the Spirit into the wilderness to be tempted of the devil. And when he had fasted forty days and forty nights, he was afterward hungered. And when the tempter came to him, he said, If thou be the Son of God, command that these stones be made bread. But he answered and said, It is written, Man shall not live by bread alone, but by every word that proceedeth out of the mouth of God. Then the devil taketh him up into the holy city, and setteth him on a pinnacle of the temple, And saith unto him, If thou be the Son of God, cast thyself down: for it is written, He shall give his angels charge concerning thee: and in their hands they shall bear thee up, lest at any time thou dash thy foot against a stone. Jesus said unto him, It is written again, Thou shalt not tempt the Lord thy God. Again, the devil taketh him up into an exceeding high mountain, and sheweth him all the kingdoms of the world, and the glory of them; And saith unto him, All these things will I give thee, if thou wilt fall down and worship me. Then saith Jesus unto him, Get thee hence, Satan: for it is written, Thou shalt worship the Lord thy God, and him only shalt thou serve. Then the devil leaveth him, and, behold, angels came and ministered unto him."*

In true God-chaser fashion, Jesus responded to Satan straight from the Word of God and that same tactic works for God chasers today. Haters will tell you that you can't do it. God chasers will respond with Philippians 4:13, *"I can do all things through Christ who strengthens me."* God chasers must believe that God's Word is true. Speaking what you don't believe is highly ineffective and counterproductive for a God chaser. God chasers must believe the Word of God, then boldly declare it in the name of Jesus. God said it and I believe it by faith. Chasing God, manifesting dreams!

Let's get back to Joseph. God gave Joseph a dream in Genesis 37 that we see come to pass in Genesis 50. But what transpired during the many years between those two chapters? I encourage you to read those complete chapters on your own, as we will only touch on key points moving forward. We know Joseph had a dream in chapter 37. Joseph shared his dream with his brothers in the same chapter and his brothers hated him. Hate can cause people to do terrible things. In Joseph's case, his brothers plotted to kill him but instead, they chose to sell him into Egyptian slavery.

Out of jealousy and pure hatred, Joseph's brothers wanted to do whatever was necessary to ensure that Joseph's dream did not come to pass. When they sold their brother into slavery, they thought they had succeeded in shutting Joseph's dream down. Little did they know they were helping set the stage for God to manifest the dream he placed inside of Joseph.

Genesis 39:1-6 says, *"And Joseph was brought down to Egypt; and Potiphar, an officer of Pharaoh, captain of the guard, an Egyptian, bought him of the hands of the Ishmeelites, which had brought him down thither. ^{2}And the LORD was with Joseph, and he was a prosperous man; and he was in the house of his master the Egyptian. ^{3}And his master saw that the LORD was with him, and that the LORD made all that he did to prosper in his hand. ^{4}And Joseph found grace in his sight, and he served him: and he made him overseer over his house, and all that he had he put into his hand. ^{5}And it came to pass from the time that he had made him overseer in his house, and over all that he had, that the LORD blessed the Egyptian's house for Joseph's sake; and the blessing of the LORD was upon all that he had in the house, and in the* *field. ⁶And he left all that he had in Joseph's hand; and he knew not ought he had, save the bread which he did eat. And Joseph was a goodly person, and well favoured."*

After reading that passage, you should be ready for another praise break. That's right, this is definitely a "Won't He do it?" moment. Will you look at God? Joseph is nearly killed by his brothers and then sold into slavery - but because of God's hand on Joseph's life and the dream He placed inside of him, Joseph prospered during his time in Egypt. Verse 6 says that this young Hebrew boy was well-favored in Egypt!

But there is always a but clause; things were just starting to look up for Joseph when trouble arose. Joseph caught the eye of Potipher's wife. Potipher was one of the Pharoah's officials. His wife made repeated advances toward Joseph. According to Genesis 39:7-12, *"And it came to pass after these things, that his master's wife cast her eyes upon Joseph; and she said, Lie with me. But he refused, and said unto his master's wife, Behold, my master wotteth not what is with me in the house, and he hath committed all that he hath to my hand; There is none greater in this house than I; neither hath he kept back anything from me but thee, because thou art his wife: how then can I do this great wickedness, and sin against God? And it came to pass, as she spake to Joseph day by day, that he hearkened not unto her, to lie by her, or to be with her. And it came to pass about this time, that Joseph went into the house to do his business; and there was none of the men of the house there within. And she caught him by his garment, saying, Lie with me: and he left his garment in her hand, and fled, and got him out."*

Potipher's wife did not stop after Joseph absconded. The drama continues in Genesis 39:13-20: *"And it came to pass, when she saw that he had left his garment in her hand, and was fled forth,*

That she called unto the men of her house, and spake unto them, saying, See, he hath brought in an Hebrew unto us to mock us; he came in unto me to lie with me, and I cried with a loud voice: And it came to pass, when he heard that I lifted up my voice and cried, that he left his garment with me, and fled, and got him out. And she laid up his garment by her, until his lord came home. And she spake unto him according to these words, saying, The Hebrew servant, which thou hast brought unto us, came in unto me to mock me: And it came to pass, as I lifted up my voice and cried, that he left his garment with me, and fled out. And it came to pass, when his master heard the words of his wife, which she spake unto him, saying, After this manner did thy servant to me; that his wrath was kindled. And Joseph's master took him, and put him into the prison, a place where the king's prisoners were bound: and he was there in the prison."

How often have the favor and blessings of God attracted unwanted attention in your life? In the case of Joseph the dreamer, this unwanted attention landed him in prison for a crime he did not commit. I want to pause here for a moment and share two quick lessons which can be gleaned from this part of Joseph's story. First, when God gives you a dream (as you can see from Joseph's story), it may not come to pass immediately. God gave Joseph the vision, but He did not share the timeline. Secondly, when God gives you a dream, it does not exempt you from obstacles and challenges. You may go through some very tough times before the dream comes to pass. But the Bible says in Romans 8:28, *"And we know that all things work together for good to them that love God, to them who are the called according to his purpose."* God chasers truly love God and know they are called according to His purpose. God chasers can be rest assured that God is present through every trial and tribulation and will move His children from dreams to manifestation in His perfect timing.

At this point in the story, Joseph is probably frustrated to say the least. He started out as his father's favorite child. As a teenager, he had a dream of greatness which displeased his brothers. After being sold into slavery in Egypt, Joseph landed in the house of the Pharaoh, where he walked in the favor of God. Soon after, he is falsely accused of trying to sleep with Potipher's wife when it was really the other way around. And now, Joseph the dreamer is sitting in prison. I am sure you know what it feels like to do the right thing yet still find yourself in a position that seems even further from your dreams.

If we fast forward a bit, we can see from Genesis 39 until Genesis 50 that God was still with Joseph. While in prison, God gave Joseph favor and allowed him to interpret a dream for the king's butler and baker. Joseph's only request was that they remember what he did for them when they were released. Of course, this would not happen for another two years. Pharaoh had a dream which no one could interpret. The Pharaoh's butler remembered Joseph and told the Pharaoh how Joseph interpreted his dream while in prison. So, the Pharaoh sends for Joseph and Joseph interprets the Pharaoh's dream. This was a task no one else in the kingdom was able to accomplish, but Joseph did it with the Lord's help and was greatly rewarded.

Joseph explained to the Pharaoh that God was showing him what was about to happen in his dream. In short, there would be seven years of plenty - followed by seven years of famine in the land. He also told Pharaoh that God was instructing him to select a wise man to help prepare for the famine – without realizing he would be the wise man chosen. In Genesis 41:40, the Pharaoh responds by selecting Joseph and stating, *"Thou shalt be over my house, and according unto thy word shall all my people be ruled: only in the throne will I be greater than thou."* In other words,

Pharaoh elevated Joseph to the position of ruler over all the land of Egypt - second only to the Pharaoh himself.

Quick question: Do you recall Joseph's dreams about everybody bowing down to him? Remember Joseph's brothers? As it turns out, when the time of famine came - Jacob, Joseph's father, sent his brothers to seek food in Egypt. Guess who they had to bow down to in order to survive the famine? Joseph - the brother they hated. Joseph - the brother they despised. Joseph - the brother they plotted to kill. Joseph – the brother they sold into slavery. Joseph the dreamer – who chased God until his dream was manifested!

In the end, Joseph was able to look his brothers in their faces and give God glory. As Joseph went through years of trials and tribulations, he did not know when or how his dream would come to pass. From his dream at age 17 to manifestation at age 39, God was orchestrating it all. God used the jealousy, the hatred, the false accusations and imprisonment to work out a greater purpose in Joseph's life. Joseph was elevated to the second highest position in all of Egypt - second only to the Pharaoh himself. Truly, God can do exceeding, abundantly above all that we can ask or think.

Dear Lord,

I come to you today to say thank you. Thank you for giving me a dream. Thank you for equipping me with the faith to see my dreams come to pass. Lord, I do not know when my dreams will manifest, but I trust in your divine timing. Thank you for being with me when I go through difficult times. Thank you for carrying me when I can't seem to find my way. Thank you for giving me the strength to hold on to my dreams in the midst of life's challenges.

Lord, I stand on your Word and believe that you are working things out in my life - good and bad, for my good. I pray for those who despise me for no reason at all - family or friends. Reveal the people in my life who mean me no good. Help me to evaluate my inner circle and walk away from anyone who might try to kill my dreams with their words or actions.

When opposition arises, help me to stand on your Word and declare it with my mouth. I am already victorious and for that, I give you praise, honor and glory. Lord, I thank you. In Jesus name, Amen.

CHAPTER 3
God Chasers Have Power

One of the most important things for you to remember as you chase God and manifest your dreams, is that you are not required to do it in your own strength or power. In the New Testament book of Acts, we find that God has given supernatural power to His children. Acts 1:1-9 says, *"The former treatise have I made, O Theophilus, of all that Jesus began both to do and teach, [2] Until the day in which he was taken up, after that he through the Holy Ghost had given commandments unto the apostles whom he had chosen: [3] To whom also he shewed himself alive after his passion by many infallible proofs, being seen of them forty days, and speaking of the things pertaining to the kingdom of God: [4] And, being assembled together with them, commanded them that they should not depart from Jerusalem, but wait for the promise of the Father, which, saith he, ye have heard of me. [5] For John truly baptized with water; but ye shall be baptized with the Holy Ghost not many days hence. [6] When they therefore were come together, they asked of him, saying, Lord, wilt thou at this time restore again the kingdom to Israel? [7] And he said unto them, It is not for you to know the times or the seasons, which the Father hath put in his own power. [8] But ye shall receive power, after that the Holy Ghost is come upon you: and ye shall be witnesses unto me both in Jerusalem, and in all Judaea, and in Samaria, and unto the uttermost part of the earth. [9] And when he had spoken these things, while they beheld, he was taken up; and a cloud received him out of their sight."*

As we consider the power of God in our lives to manifest our dreams, I would like to focus on verse 8 of the aforementioned scripture, *"But ye shall receive power, after that the Holy Ghost is come upon you: and ye shall be witnesses unto me both in Jerusalem, and in all Judaea, and in Samaria, and unto the uttermost part of the earth."* God said in His Word that we shall we receive POWER. Aren't you glad you do not have to do this alone? Not only is God with you, but according to the Book of Acts - He is giving you power. Let's take a closer look at the book of Acts.

Within the 28 chapters of Acts, we find invaluable information about the development of the early church immediately following the death, burial and resurrection of our Lord and Savior Jesus Christ. Covering approximately 32 years - around AD 30, when Jesus ascended to heaven until AD 62 when it is believed the Apostle Paul was imprisoned in Rome, Acts tells us much about the spread of the Gospel from Jerusalem to Rome. How did this growth happen; through the power of the Holy Spirit.

The Holy Spirit is a central figure in the book of Acts and is mentioned nearly 60 times throughout the entire book. This mention of the Holy Spirit starts with Jesus' final words to the disciples before He ascends into heaven. There we see Jesus the Risen Christ, God incarnate or God in the flesh, the Messiah, the Son of the Living God; gathered together in Jerusalem with His disciples. Clearly Jesus is alive and well, having convinced the disciples over the course of 40 days after His crucifixion, that He has truly risen from the dead. As Jesus nears the end of His earthly mission - before He returns to God the Father in heaven, He instructs the disciples to stay in Jerusalem and wait for the promise of the Holy Ghost. Jesus then told the disciples they would be baptized with the Holy Ghost and would receive power after the Holy Ghost had come upon them.

So where does this power come from and how can God chasers benefit? How can this power help you manifest your dreams? Let's bookmark the book of Acts and hop over to Genesis. The opening words of the Holy Bible in Genesis 1:1 state that "...*In the beginning, God created...*" This means that God was present in time and space before creation itself. Throughout the entire Bible - from the Old Testament to the New Testament, we find scriptures to support the fact that God is the creator and sovereign ruler of all things and that He can do whatever He wants to do. God is omnipotent. So when we consider the origin of the power God gives to those who chase after Him, we should look no further than the Almighty God. Adonai - My Great Lord. El Roi, the God who sees me. El Shaddai, the All-sufficient one. Jehovah, the self-existent one. Jehovah Rapha, The Lord who heals. Jehovah Rohi, The Lord is my shepherd. Jehovah Tsidkenu, The Lord our Righteousness. Elohim - The All Powerful One. Clearly, God is the source of the power He promises to God chasers in Acts and this power will equip us to manifest our dreams.

But that is not it. See, there is something that is described in the Synoptic Gospels of Matthew, Mark and Luke. There is something that happened over 2,000 years ago; after God omnipotent encapsulated all of His splendor, glory, power and divinity into the flesh and blood of His only begotten Son and came down through 42 generations to give us abundant life. Jesus - the second person of the Trinity, God incarnate; shed His blood on the cross at Calvary for you and me. That is the seemingly bad news, but we all know the truth. Jesus died - but He died with a purpose. He died that we might have life. Moreover, His death was not permanent - for the Word of God tells us that on the third day, He rose with what? He rose with all power in His hands.

So now we have been reminded that God the Father - the first person in the trinity, is all-powerful. We know that Jesus the Christ - the second person in the trinity, is also all-powerful Well, what about the Holy Spirit we started talking about earlier? How does the Holy Spirit – the third person in the Trinity – fit into this story?

I am glad you asked. According to the Harper Collins Bible Dictionary, the Holy Spirit is defined as: 'The mysterious power or presence of God that operates within individuals and communities, inspiring or empowering them with qualities they would not otherwise possess'. The term 'spirit' translates Hebrew 'Ruakh' and Greek 'Pneuma' - words denoting 'wind', 'breath' and by extension, a life-giving element. With the adjective 'holy', the reference is to the divine spirit - i.e. the Spirit of God.

Here is an illustration that I love to use. As I was trying to figure out how to explain this last part, God reminded me of my cell phone. Most people have cell phones today and cell phones today are certainly smart, aren't they? In fact, they're not called cell phones anymore –they are called smart phones. Back in the day, we used phones to make calls, but nowadays, smart phones can do tremendously more than just make phone calls. These highly-intelligent, new gadgets are like mini computers. They are sleek and shiny on the outside and come pre-loaded with tons of information, apps - plus many other amazing things which are downloaded into their operating systems.

If you own a smart phone, you know exactly what I mean. I use my cell phone for everything; it does everything short of cooking dinner and cleaning my house. I can use my cell phone to make calls, send text messages, Skype, Facebook, Instagram, Twitter read my bible, read books and magazines, track my steps or mileage when I run, listen to music, pay bills, buy shoes, watch movies – the list is endless. Again, this phone can do any and everything...as long as it's charged.

      See, as fantabulous (my special word) as these devices are, they are quite similar to us. They can't function or live up to their full capacity if they are not fully charged. So, when you first get your smart phone - you connect it to a USB cord, which is connected to an electrical outlet. The electricity flows from the outlet through the USB cord to the smart phone, allowing it to charge – but it doesn't stop there. Every night, you have to repeat this process. You connect the phone to the USB cord that is connected to the power source or outlet - then the electricity flows from the power source through the USB cord to the cell phone so that it can charge. Let's pretend for a moment that we are a cell phone in need of a charge. How do we get powered up? Well, connect the cell phone (that's you) to the Power Source (God) through the USB cord (Jesus Christ). Then the POWER of God (the Holy Spirit) flows through the USB cord (Jesus the Christ) into the cell phone (that's you again) as the power of God is released and you are fully charged (or filled with the power of the Holy Ghost). Now, you are ready to operate in your pre-loaded gifts, walk in your God-given anointing, and experience the manifestation of what God downloaded into your very being while you were still in your mother's womb!

      You already know what comes next. Every God chaser should pause to give God praise right now for the Holy Spirit and His ability to manifest your dreams through the power of God. INSERT PRAISE BREAK HERE! God has given you a huge dream. You are aware the dream came from God because you have been chasing God and you know His voice - yet you still long for manifestation. You have not seen your dream come to pass because you're attempting to do it in your own strength and power.

Here is my advice (of course, there is a prayer at this end of this chapter, but we cannot wait that long); there is no more time to waste. Repeat these words right now, then repeat this exercise every single day for the next 30 days: "I am a child of the Most-High God. I am connected to God through my relationship with Jesus Christ. I have access to God's power – the mysterious power of God also known as the Holy Ghost. I am a God chaser and I have the Holy Ghost power that is necessary to manifest my God-given dreams."

This is not just any old, ordinary power. The word 'power' in Acts 1:8 stems from the Greek word dunamis. It's where the English words dynamite and dynamo are derived. So, when we talk about power in this verse, we are talking about dunamis power – God's explosive power. This power enables us to boldly chase after God and allows us to live a life sold-out for God. It is this power, which enables us to perform great and mighty acts for God. It is this dunamis power that allows us to resist sin. It is this power that enables God chasers to manifest their dreams.

Jesus told the disciples they would receive this POWER - dunamis power and that they would be witnesses in Jerusalem, in all of Judaea, in Samaria and unto the earth. That same power is available to every born-again Believer who has responded to God's way of salvation as found in Romans 10:9, *"That if thou shalt confess with thy mouth the Lord Jesus, and shalt believe in thine heart that God hath raised him from the dead, thou shalt be saved."* It is imperative to remember that once you are connected to Jesus Christ, you have access to God and the Holy Spirit.

God Chasers Have Power

Once you are connected to God, you can stay connected by chasing after Him. Keep praying. Keep fasting. Keep reading God's word. Keep giving your time, talent and treasure. Keep worshipping God. Keep offering God praise. Keep thanking God for the dreams He placed inside of you and keep chasing Him until the dream has come to fruition.

No matter how big or difficult you think it will be to make your dream happen - you have the power to do it in Jesus' name. Perhaps you want to start a non-profit organization to serve victims of sex trafficking, drug abuse or homelessness. As a God chaser, you have the power to take your city by storm and make a difference in your community. Perhaps God has given you a vision for launching a new ministry or church. As a God chaser, you have the power to share the love of Jesus Christ and boldly proclaim the Good News to those who need to hear it most. Maybe you are unemployed but have a dream of launching your own business. As a God chaser, you have the power according to Romans 4:17 to "...*speak those things which be not as though they were.*" Your dream may be to lead your spouse to Christ. As a God chaser, you have the power to minister to your husband or wife. God chasers have the power to manifest dreams!

The Spirit of God dwells in every God chaser. The very same spirit that raised Jesus from the dead is living inside of every born-again Believer right now. You have power. But where can we find this power you ask? There is power in the name of Jesus. You don't have to live life in defeat nor do you have to remain in bondage to anything not in alignment with God's will for your life. Jesus came to you free and because of His victory over death on the cross, you have power.

There is power in the Word of God. John 1:1 says *"In the beginning was the Word, and the Word was with God and the Word was God."* John 1:14 tells us that *"The Word was made flesh, and dwelt among us, (and we beheld His glory, the glory as of the only begotten of the Father,) full of grace and truth."* There is also power in the Word of God, because Jesus is the Word made flesh and Jesus has all power - which means as joint heirs with Christ, God chasers have power.

There is power in your tongue. Now, this can be dangerous because the Bible says in Proverbs 18:21, *"Death and life are in the power of the tongue: and they that love it shall eat the fruit thereof."* Be very careful with how you use this power. You can use the power of your tongue to build up or you can use the power of your tongue to tear down. Your haters use the power of the tongue to tear down your dreams. Make a decision to use the creative power of your tongue to speak life. Speak life over your family, your career, your ministry, your money, your health, your business and your dreams! You have power!

There is power in our praise. The Bible tells us in Acts 16:25-26, *"And at midnight Paul and Silas prayed, and sang praises unto God: and the prisoners heard them. And suddenly there was a great earthquake, so that the foundations of the prison were shaken: and immediately all the doors were opened, and every one's bands were loosed."* When you clap your hands in praise, you experience the power of God. When you stomp your feet in praise, you experience the power of God. When you open your mouth to cry out to God in adoration and praise, you experience the power of God. Miracles occur when we praise God.

There is power in our prayers. The Word of God says in James 5:16, *"The effectual fervent prayer of a righteous man availeth much."* God never intended for you to do it by yourself. God says in Matthew 18:20, *"For where two or three are gathered together in my name, there am I in the midst of them."* He is present in your prayers and your prayers are full of the power of God. You have the power to manifest what God has placed inside of you.

Remember that God is omnipotent. God knew that you would need someone to keep you charged. He knew you needed someone to fan the flames. He knew that you would need someone to reignite your dreams and catapult you into manifestation. That is why Jesus promised to send the Holy Spirit to us in the book of Acts. He knew that once He ascended to heaven to sit at the right hand of God and intercede on our behalf, we would need the power of the Holy Spirit to sustain us as we live a life pleasing to God. He knew that we needed the power of the Holy Spirit to live our destiny. He knew that we needed the power of the Holy Spirit to fulfill the dreams He placed within us. He knew we needed the power of the Holy Spirit to reach our full potential. He knew that we needed the power of the Holy Spirit to be witnesses throughout the land.

And so God freely releases His power to His children so that we can get charged, empowered and fired up to do His will on earth. When we run low on juice; when we operate with only one power cell, when we are not living the abundant life God promised in His Word - all we have to do is reconnect to the source of our power and resume chasing God.

There is power - supernatural, Holy Ghost power- dwelling inside of us. If you are going to chase God and manifest your dreams - you must know beyond a shadow of doubt, that you have power. Here are a few more declarations that are pretty powerful (pun intended):

- I am a God chaser with power. I know I have power, because God promised me in Acts 1:8 that I "would receive power."
- I am a God chaser with power. I know I have power because I see the power of God manifest in my life each and every day.
- I am a God chaser with power. I know I have power because my God is All-Powerful and I am a joint-heir to that power through Jesus Christ.
- I am a God chaser with power. I know I have power because I am a God chaser and I am manifesting my dreams.

Dear Lord,

I first want to thank you for saving me. I thank you God that your Son Jesus Christ, died on the cross to save me from my sins. I thank you that God rose Jesus from the dead with all power in His hands. And because Jesus died and rose again, the debt of my sins have been paid in full.

Thank you for allowing me to connect with you, through your Son Jesus Christ. Thank you for allowing the power of God to flow to me through your precious Holy Spirit. The same power that rose Jesus from the dead dwells in me.

Lord help me to realize the power that you have given me to manifest my dreams. Help me to activate the power of God in my life that I might see my dreams begin to manifest.

I thank you for your love. I thank you for your grace and mercy. I thank you for saving me. Thank you for giving me power! Let me use it for your glory. In Jesus name, Amen.

CHAPTER 4
Be Strong and Courageous

I recently preached a message on the Old Testament book of Joshua that was completely life-changing for me. As I prepared my message, I realized that my approach to chasing God had been completely wrong. I found that within the first chapter of Joshua, God provides critical information about chasing God and manifesting dreams. It is right there as plain as day - yet until recently, I missed it. Some might say, it was hidden in plain sight. Today, I want to share with you what the Lord showed me about chasing God and manifesting your dreams.

Let's look at Joshua 1:1-9, "Now after the death of Moses the servant of the Lord it came to pass, that the Lord spake unto Joshua the son of Nun, Moses' minister, saying, Moses my servant is dead; now therefore arise, go over this Jordan, thou, and all this people, unto the land which I do give to them, even to the children of Israel. Every place that the sole of your foot shall tread upon, that have I given unto you, as I said unto Moses. From the wilderness and this Lebanon even unto the great river, the river Euphrates, all the land of the Hittites, and unto the great sea toward the going down of the sun, shall be your coast. There shall not any man be able to stand before thee all the days of thy life: as I was with Moses, so I will be with thee: I will not fail thee, nor forsake thee. Be strong and of a good courage: for unto this people shalt thou divide for an inheritance the land, which I sware unto their fathers to give them. Only be thou strong and very courageous, that thou mayest observe to do according to all the law, which Moses my servant commanded thee: turn not from it to the right hand or to the left, that thou mayest prosper whithersoever thou goest. This book of the law shall not depart out of thy mouth; but thou shalt meditate therein day and night, that thou mayest observe to do according to all that is written therein: for then thou shalt make thy way prosperous, and then thou shalt have good success. Have not I commanded thee? Be strong and of a good courage; be not afraid, neither be thou dismayed: for the Lord thy God is with thee whithersoever thou goest."

And that, my dear God chaser, is the key to effectively chasing God. If you are anything like me, you may not have caught the secret just yet. Let's dig a little deeper into those verses. Joshua starts right on the heels of Moses's death in Deuteronomy. Deuteronomy 34:5-7 says *"So Moses the servant of the Lord died there in the land of Moab, according to the word of the Lord. And he buried him in a valley in the land of Moab, over against Beth-peor: but no man knoweth of his sepulchre unto this day. And Moses was a hundred and twenty years old when he died: his eye was not dim, nor his natural force abated."*

Picture the scene: Moses is now dead and the people are mourning the loss of their leader. God used Moses to deliver the Pharoah. God used Moses to deliver the people of God from Egyptian bondage. God used Moses to miraculously carry Israel across the Red Sea on dry ground. God used Moses to lead Israel through the wilderness. God used Moses to present the Law and God used Moses to carry the people of God to the promised land. However, we know from scripture that Moses himself was not to cross over into the land of promise. He died just before the people were ready to enter the promised land, leaving God to raise another leader by the name of Joshua.

Imagine how Joshua must have felt when Moses died. I am sure Joshua was devastated. The death of Moses was devastating for everyone. Deuteronomy 34:8 says, *"And the children of Israel wept for Moses in the plains of Moab thirty days: so the days of weeping and mourning for Moses were ended."* No one considered the idea of entering the land of promise without their fearless leader Moses, especially his beloved assistant Joshua.

Have you ever lost someone whom you respected and admired? Have you ever experienced the loss of a great teacher, mentor or coach you hoped would be with you forever, although you knew that wasn't possible? Over the past two years, I lost two of my spiritual mentors: Chaplain Denise Dinkins and Deacon William Eubanks, both of the Mount Airy Church of God in Christ in Philadelphia. Just like Joshua and the children of Israel, I was devastated by both deaths because these two individuals played such an important role in my spiritual development.

Chaplain Dinkins was an amazing woman of God. She was a teacher, preacher, prayer intercessor, counselor and much more. Chaplain Dinkins facilitated the pre-marital counseling classes for me and my husband during our engagement and we continued to seek Chaplain Dinkins' marital advice long after we were married. Chaplain Dinkins helped me discern my call into ministry. I spent time with Chaplain Dinkins interceding for others on our church prayer line. Chaplain Dinkins also taught me everything I know about spiritual warfare and deliverance ministry. Her wisdom, spiritual guidance, encouragement and prayers helped shape me into the woman of God I am today. Now she is gone.

Deacon William Eubanks had the same impact on my life. Although I'd heard of Deacon Eubanks, I did not formally make his acquaintance until I took a class he was teaching at the Mt. Airy Religious Training Institute (MARTI). I started in Deacon Eubanks' class on cults and world religions. My husband and I also took a course on the Revelation taught by Deacon Eubanks. We later joined Deacon Eubanks' Sunday school class. Just like Jesus, Deacon Eubanks was unapologetic about his Father's business. He did not waste time with frivolous talk or gossip. When Deacon Eubanks opened his mouth, you better believe God had given him something to say.

I remember so clearly the day Deacon Eubanks called me with a message from God regarding my call into ministry. My youngest daughter Kaitlyn was just a toddler. During that call, God used Deacon Eubanks to encourage me to apply for seminary at the Lutheran Theological Seminary at Philadelphia. The decision to attend seminary was something I had been struggling with for some time. I knew God had called me to go to seminary. In fact, I actually started the application process for seminary a few years prior, but I did not complete my application because I soon discovered I was pregnant with Kaitlyn. As I sought the Lord to discern when I should pursue seminary again, God spoke through Deacon Eubanks. Deacon Eubanks was excited when I responded to God's call. He wrote my recommendation letter and blessed God the day I was accepted. He even gave me his box of Greek flash cards to assist me in my class on koine Greek.

I talked to Deacon Eubanks throughout my years in seminary, sometimes about my classes and sometimes about my life. He encouraged me to keep pressing, to pray and fast and to see myself graduating. When the time came for me to preach my initial sermon, Deacon Eubanks was there to watch God use me. Although he was unable to attend my graduation in 2013, I talked to him after graduation and he was well aware of how God was moving in my life. He was very proud of my growth and my surrender to the Lord's will.

Chaplain Dinkins and Deacon Eubanks were to me, what Moses was to Joshua - therefore I can relate to how Joshua felt when Moses died. I can feel the sense of sadness and pain Joshua suffered knowing that he had to complete the next leg of his spiritual journey without the leader God used to groom him. I can feel Joshua's uncertainty. I can feel Joshua's fear and can only imagine all of the questions racing through his mind.

God, in His omniscience, knew how Joshua was feeling after the death of Moses. God also knew what Joshua would have to face as He elevated him to a position of leadership over the people of Israel. As Moses' assistant, Joshua had certainly learned about seeking God's face, walking with God and trusting and obeying God. God was transitioning Joshua from being a servant of Moses, to a direct servant of God; a position that, perhaps unbeknownst to Joshua, he was training for his entire life.

In the first chapter of Joshua, God speaks directly to him for the very first time, sharing words of encouragement and instruction. First, He acknowledged the death of Moses and told Joshua and the people of God to rise and go into the land of promise. Second, God reminded Joshua of all the land and territory included in that promise. Third, God encourages Joshua. He assures Joshua that He will stay with him as He did for Moses and promises not to leave Joshua. Fourth, He commands Joshua to be strong and courageous.

Now here's where it gets really good. Remember that we are searching for the hidden treasure in this chapter - one of the secrets of effectively chasing after God. The first thing that stood out to me was God's instruction to Joshua to be strong and courageous. Had God only said it once, I probably wouldn't have paid much attention. But as I studied this chapter repeatedly - I noticed God told Joshua to be strong and courageous three times! Therefore, I knew this command was important.

Clearly, God knew the task in store for Joshua and I am pretty sure Joshua had reservations. After all, Joshua served for years under the leadership of Moses. Joshua was Moses' assistant - his right-hand guy. But now with the death of Moses, God was elevating Joshua to a position of authority and assigned him to lead the people of God into Canaan to defeat enemies and possess the land.

While I can appreciate God's instructions to Joshua to be strong and courageous, I also found it disturbing. In fact, those words – which were repeated three times, frustrated me. I thought about how I'd feel if I were in Joshua's shoes. Then I remembered I actually have been in Joshua's shoes. In fact, I am walking in his footsteps right now as I deal with the loss of Chaplain Dinkins and Deacon Eubanks.

I would love to follow God's command to be strong and courageous, but my big question is how? How God? How am I supposed to be strong and courageous after all that has happened? How am I supposed to be strong and courageous after everything that's been done to me? How am I supposed to be strong and courageous when I am facing so much ahead? How am I supposed to be strong and courageous when I know the enemy is trying to kill me? How am I supposed to be strong and courageous when I am so ill-equipped?

If you've ever felt like this, then Joshua 1:8 will bless you. Joshua 1:8 says, *"This book of the law shall not depart out of thy mouth; but thou shalt meditate therein day and night, that thou mayest observe to do according to all that is written therein: for then thou shalt make thy way prosperous, and then thou shalt have good success."* Did you get it? This is another shouting moment. Read that verse again.

In Joshua 1:8 - not only does God share the key to being strong and courageous, He also shares the key to prosperity and success! It's all about reading, meditating, speaking and acting on the Word of God! Now, sometimes it may be easier said than done, but that's it - plain and simple. We have to keep the Word of God near us and meditate on it day and night.

How do you meditate on God's Word? Well, meditating on the Word of God is more than simply going to church and reading a passage of scripture during Sunday service. Meditating on the Word of God is more than just reading your daily scripture email every morning. Meditating on the Word of God is more than just checking off 'Bible reading' from your to-do list. Meditating on the Word of God means reading passages repeatedly in order to gain clarity and understanding.

Meditating on the Word of God means spending time in the word of God. Meditating on the word of God is thoughtful reflection. Meditating on the Word of God means asking God questions about what you are reading: Lord, what does this passage mean? Lord, how is this passage relevant today? Lord, what did you intend for me to take away from this story? Lord, how can I apply this principle to my life?

Another key to meditating on the Word is declaring it with your mouth. As I thought about this idea, I was reminded of my favorite childhood book, "The Little Engine that Could." In short, there was a tiny little engine faced with a task that no other engine was willing to do. The engine had to carry a large load of toys up and over a huge mountain. The little engine decided that what seemed impossible was possible and began the journey up the mountain. As the engine moved forward in faith, it repeated the following words, "I think I can." The engine kept repeating that phrase over and over again as it climbed the huge mountain and before realizing it - the engine successfully climbed all the way up the mountain.

So, God told Joshua to be strong and courageous and gave him instruction. As you will see throughout the rest of the story, God stood by His Word. He remained with Joshua, leading and guiding him. He gave Joshua effective strategies for conquering his enemies and taking possession of the land God promised to the children of Israel. As long as Joshua followed God's command, he prospered and found success – no matter how great the challenges.

When faced with tasks too big for handling in our own strength, we must act like that little engine. Moreover, we should be like Joshua. We have to speak the Word of God over our lives and our situation. We have to meditate on the Word of God day and night and we must do what God instructs in His Word. If we do these things, God says we will prosper and be successful!

Your dream may seem far-fetched and impossible right now. Your dream may seem bigger than anything you have ever done in your life. You might believe that you lack the knowledge, wisdom, experience, talent or resources to bring it to fruition. Guess what? All of that is probably true, however nothing is impossible to the God you are chasing, my fellow God chaser. God equips those who chase after Him. Stop looking at the gigantic task or obstacle and look at God. As a God chaser, you are already meditating on the Word of God daily; as a God chaser, you are already doing everything the Bible instructs. Therefore, you are doing your part. Now, move out of the way and let God do His part. Let Him grant you prosperity and success in accordance with His Word.

Dear God,

You are God Almighty. You are omniscient, omnipotent and omnipresent and for that, I give your name praise. Thank you for walking with me. Thank you for talking to me. Thank you for your Word. Lord help me to be disciplined in spending time reading, studying and meditating on your word. Help me to look to you when I am faced with obstacles that threaten to kill my dreams. Help me to meditate on your Word day and night.

Thank you Lord for illuminating your Word. Thank you for revealing the secret to prosperity and success. Thank you for giving me tools to help me continue chasing after you and manifesting the dreams that you placed inside of me. I will be strong and courageous. I am a God chaser and I will manifest my dreams. In Jesus' name, Amen.

CHAPTER 5
On the Run

A few years ago, music power couple Beyoncé and Jay-Z hosted a tour entitled 'On the Run.' As I thought about what it means to be a God chaser, I concluded that God chasers are on the run as well. Disclaimer: I have no idea if Beyoncé and Jay-Z were running *from* someone or something - *to* someone, something or both. However, I do believe that God chasers are running away from sin and running to Jesus. Let's look at Hebrews 12:1 to elucidate my claim: *"Wherefore seeing we also are compassed about with so great a cloud of witnesses, let us lay aside every weight, and the sin which doth so easily beset us, and let us run with patience the race that is set before us."*

The book of Hebrews is a go-to resource for all God chasers, especially Hebrews 11. Written by an unknown Christian, Hebrews is home to some of the most powerful scriptures about faith in the entire Bible. In Hebrews 11:1, we learn that *"...faith is the substance of things hoped for, the evidence of things not seen."* In Hebrews 11:6, we learn that *"...without faith, it is impossible to please Him; for he that cometh to God must believe that He is, and that He is a rewarder of them that diligently seek Him."* The remainder of Hebrews 11 continues the faith theme with numerous examples of individuals who are part of the role-call of faith.

As we examine Hebrews 12:1 in the context of chasing God and manifesting your dreams, there are several things to point out - key words that will be important as we move forward in this verse. The first word to highlight is 'wherefore' (or 'therefore' in some translations). Now, let's return to grammar school briefly: in the English language, 'therefore' is a conjunctive adverb - a type of adverb connecting two independent clauses or sentences. This means that the translators of this scripture want the reader to understand there is a connection between what we read in Hebrews 12:1 and the preceding chapter.

Review Hebrews 12:1 again: *"Wherefore seeing we also are compassed about with so great a cloud of witnesses, let us lay aside every weight, and the sin which doth so easily beset us, and let us run with patience the race that is set before us."* Without the context provided in Hebrews 11, the reader will struggle to understand the reference to the cloud of witnesses. The use of the conjunctive adverb in Hebrews 12:1, prompts us to return to Hebrews 11 and receive clarity regarding what the author is actually saying in the beginning of Hebrews 12.

Before we delve into the 'cloud of witnesses,' I'll break down the key directives in Hebrews 12:1 so that the context is clear. If we focus on the main idea, the writer tells us that we are surrounded by a cloud of witnesses and instructs us to do two things: lay down every weight and sin and run the race. The author is using race imagery to make his point. In fact, to be specific - the author is referring to the Greek races of his time. Greek athletes ran in large stadiums surrounded by spectators or witnesses, much like today's athletes. What do spectators do at games; they cheer and encourage the athletes to keep going. The unknown writer in Hebrews paints a picture of athletes running a race in a big stadium, surrounded by witnesses (spectators and fans) who are cheering the runners on and encouraging them as they head to the finish line.

Now for the 'cloud of witnesses': long before Beyoncé and Jay Z were on the run, long before Bonnie and Clyde were on the run - even before you and I were on the run, there was a cloud of witnesses on the run, chasing after God. If we hop back to Hebrews 11 - the chapter connected to Hebrews 12 by the conjunctive adverb 'therefore', we realize that the cloud of witnesses described in Hebrews 11 are the heroes of faith. Starting in Hebrews 11:7, we are reminded how Noah – who'd never seen a drop of rain fall from the sky in his LIFE, was obedient to God and built the ark to save his family and humankind by faith. Noah was on the run.

In Hebrews 11:7-9, we see how Abraham chose to obey God by leaving his homeland, (having no idea where he was going) by faith. Abraham was on the run. In verse 11, we find that by faith, Sara received strength to conceive a son when she was past child-bearing age. Sarah was on the run. And in the remaining verses, we discover the faith which Abraham clung to when he prepared to sacrifice his only son – the one who was promised to him in obedience to God. Abraham was on the run.

We learn of Moses' faith story from the time he was born, until God used him to part the Red Sea and deliver the children of Israel from Egyptian bondage. Moses was on the run. We learn how the wall of Jericho came crumbling down by faith under the leadership of Joshua. Joshua was on the run. And what about Rahab helping the spies by faith? Rahab is one of many examples of God using imperfect people to do His will. Rahab was previously known as a harlot - but her faith transitioned her from harlotry to the lineage of Jesus Christ and inclusion into the role-call of faith. Rahab was on the run.

Hebrews 11 ends by stating there isn't enough room to name every hero of faith. The cloud of witnesses is too large for the confinement of that chapter. The author names a few more people; Gideon, Barack, Sampson, David and Samuel who were all part of the cloud of witnesses surrounding every believer on the run, chasing after God and manifesting dreams.

One thing I like about chasing after God - unlike running a physical race, is that you don't need sneakers or running gear and aren't required to be in a certain place. You can chase after God right where you are. All you need is a relationship with God, through his Son Jesus Christ to start your race. But the Hebrew author - as we saw earlier, offers great tips on running the race. This is what we'll examine next.

The Hebrew author tells us in Hebrews 12:1 to "...*lay aside every weight and sin that doth so easily beset us.*" God's Word translation says, we must "...*get rid of everything that slows us down, especially sin that distracts us.*" Let's review weights and sin. In biblical times, people carried pouches with weights. The weights were used as forms of measurement. Items of known weight were put on one side of a scale and used to determine the weight of the other item. A weight in the spiritual realm might be a sin, but doesn't have to be a sin. Just as a weight slows down or even stops your progress in the natural, it is the same in the spiritual.

Sin in its simplest form, is disobedience to God. If God tells you to say or do something but you don't, you are sinning (rebelling) against God. You are disobeying God. The same goes for times when God tells you not to say or do something. If you still say or do it - you are in sin. Weights and sins can disrupt your pursuit of God and block the manifestation of your dreams.

Again, the Hebrews author tells us to lay aside every weight and sin. Laying aside means more than just putting something down. The idea of laying something aside in Greek was used to describe the removal of clothing. Why does the author use this type of imagery? Well, remember the earlier reference to Greek athleticism? The author is at it again; Greek athletes often raced in the nude. This was not a sexual action, but rather a way of stripping themselves of anything hindering their race performance.

Let's be clear - I am not suggesting that anyone should take off their clothes to go streaking. However, as a God chaser - I want you to understand that you are on the run and it's your responsibility to remove weights or sins that disrupt or block the manifestation of your dreams. Think about that for a moment. What would happen if you removed weight and sin from your life? What is hindering your run right now? What is stopping you from being all that God desires? What is disrupting your run as you chase after God? What is blocking the manifestation of your dream? Money? Pride? Ego? Rebellion? Fear? Doubt? Disobedience? Worry?

If you are going to chase after God, you have to run as the Hebrew author instructed. You have to lay aside those weights and sins. Take it off in Jesus' name. Strip your life of anything hindering your walk with God. Get rid of anything that blocks your blessing and when you feel like giving up, remember the cloud of witnesses – past and present, who are cheering you on and excitedly waiting for you to cross the finish line.

Now that we've talked about the cloud of witnesses, weights and sins - let me share a few tips on how to run your race with patience. First, I want you to remember this: your race, God's pace. I run with an awesome group of women called Black Girls Run and our mantra is 'Your race, Your pace'. The reason we cling to that mantra is because running is personal and unique to each individual. The only thing runners have in common with each other is the desire to cross the finish line. Everything else is personal.

As a runner, I come with my own life experience. I come with my own training. I come with my own level of fitness. I come with my own level of preparedness or lack thereof. As I am running, I do not have time to be concerned with anyone else. I do not care who is ahead or behind me.

My race gets even better as a God chaser. My race as a God chaser is personal, due to my personal relationship with Jesus Christ. My race as a God chaser comes with training in the form of God's Word. My race as a God chaser comes with preparation through praise, worship, prayer and Bible study. As a God chaser, I do not worry about the competition, because there is none. It does not matter who is up front or behind me, because every single person who calls on the name of the Lord Jesus Christ is running a race that has already been won! You know the drill. Pause for praise right now!

God chasers will manifest their dreams in God's perfect timing. All you have to do is run your race, God's pace. Stop looking at everyone else and focus on yourself. You do not know what the person on the left or right has experienced in order to get where they are and you don't need to know because their race is not yours. They are chasing God at the pace He prescribed for them. You should chase God at the pace prescribed for you. When you are chasing after God, remember that God is your coach. God is the one leading, guiding and keeping you on track. You may not be where you want to be, but you are exactly where God wants you to be. Your race, God's pace.

The second point I want to make about running this race with patience is trusting your trainer. My runner friends say trust your training. However, God chasers realize it really isn't the training we should trust, but rather the trainer. As you chase after God, you will face challenges and obstacles along the way. As a runner, I've frequently been caught off guard by excessive heat or cold, steep hills, uneven pavement, rain, ice and more - but because of my training, I've always been able to persevere. I didn't wait until race day to start the training that my trainer prescribed. I trained in advance, so that when the unexpected happened - I was prepared. That's what you must do when you are chasing after God. You must trust God and follow the training plan He provided for you in His Word.

Do not be afraid and do not be discouraged. You may not have expected the challenges you are facing on the path to fulfilling your dreams. But God knew and God planned a way for you to overcome them. God wants you to be strong and courageous just like Joshua. He wants you to remember that He is with you and will never leave your nor forsake you. The race is fixed and you have already won. All you have to do is keep chasing God.

Dear Lord,

I thank you for the examples of faith that are found in your Word. I thank you for the cloud of witnesses who are now cheering me on as I run my race at your pace. I ask that you would help me to identify any weights or sins that are hindering my run as I chase after you. Lord, help me to lay them down in accordance with your Word. I repent right now of any sin that is hindering my run. I ask that you would help me stop comparing myself to everyone around me and focus on you. And Lord, help me to remember that the race is already won. I am victorious. I am a God chaser and I will manifest the dreams that you have placed inside of me. In Jesus' name, Amen.

CHAPTER 6
Dream Haters

God chasers must be vigilant and beware of dream haters at all times. Dream haters will try to kill your dreams in order to prevent manifestation. The story of Joseph presents a great case study on dream haters. I will not outline the entire story of Joseph again, but using Joseph and his brothers - plus my own personal story as examples, I want to discuss how dream haters appear and how God chasers can respond in order to manifest their dreams.

The Bible says that God gave Joseph a dream, yet there is no mention of God giving Joseph's brothers any dreams. When Joseph shared his dream with his brothers, they hated him. I have preached on this biblical story in the past, however I always focused on the dream's content. Joseph's brothers hated Joseph because in his dream, he was in a position of authority over his brothers, who were bowing down to him. I guess that type of dream might make anyone jealous and angry. However, it was not only the content of the dream that caused Joseph's brothers to hate him – but also the fact that Joseph was the only one who was given a dream. Some dream haters will hate your dream simply because you have a dream and they do not.

There is another group of dream haters, but they weren't always dream haters - they used to be dreamers just like you. They had their own dreams, but never took action to make their dreams come true. Over time, their dreams remained just that; dreams, without any manifestation - and dreamers without manifestation eventually get frustrated and angry. They attempt to project their negative feelings and emotions onto God chasers who dare to dream, chase God and actually live their God-given dreams.

Another reason why dream haters emerge is because they believe your dreams will actually come true. Think about Joseph's dream again; although the dream may have been offensive to his brothers, if they believed it was only a dream - they probably would not have responded as they did. When Joseph's brothers heard his dream, they knew it came from God and that it would happen. That is why they immediately tried to kill Joseph, in hopes of killing the dream as well.

How many times have you shared a dream with someone who responded negatively? You thought this person would be excited about your dreams, but they had nothing good to say. You walk away feeling angry, hurt and unsupported by people you thought really believed in you. Here is the deal: while it's natural to feel angry or hurt by someone's response to your dream - do not for one minute assume that person doesn't believe in your dreams. I suspect it is just the opposite; dream haters absolutely believe in you and your dreams. While they may say things like "that is stupid" or "that will never happen," what they believe in their heart is that your dreams will absolutely come to pass. They cannot stand the idea of watching you soar while they remain in the same place.

Often, dream haters will see things in you which you may not see in yourself. Dream haters can see how God is moving in your life and where He is taking you. Joseph's brothers were afraid that Joseph's dream would happen. How many times were you in a position where God was elevating you and it seemed like the haters just started coming out of the wood work? This happens because they hear your dream and know where God is taking you. They recognize the power and authority of God in your life and they can't stand it. They believe in your dreams just as much as you and knowing that your dreams will manifest while their dreams remain unfilled, enrages them.

Dream haters are like Satan - the enemy of our soul. Dream haters watch you closely. Dream haters see everything going on in your life. Dream haters are watching God move in your life. Dream haters are watching God use you. Dream haters are watching God bless you. Dream haters are watching God pour into your life. Dream haters are watching God open doors for you. Dream haters are watching God anoint you. Dream haters are watching God elevate you. They despise this because they want it all for themselves.

Dream haters had big dreams once, but never pressed through to realize those dreams. They allowed life to get in the way. They let circumstances and situations stop them from moving forward. They let fear creep in and gave in to excuses. But here you are, with your God- chasing self actually pursuing your dream to their dismay. They hate you simply because you have the audacity to pursue the dream God gave you. I talked about this briefly in the earlier chapters. God gives us dreams and we have a responsibility to act on what He places in our hearts so that they will come to pass. There is nothing special about dreaming, however it requires bold faith and action to pursue a dream. Dream haters hate your boldness and your actions!

The good news is that there are plenty of ways to avoid becoming a victim of a dream hater. The first course of action is to become a God chaser. There is no match for a God chaser on the path to manifesting his or her dreams. The haters may try, but won't succeed. Clearly, Joseph is a great example. The one thing which kept Joseph through everything he experienced was his relationship with God. Joseph was a God chaser and Joseph's dream was manifested. If you chase after God, you too will manifest the dream He gave you. Remember Isaiah 54:17, *"No weapon that is formed against thee shall prosper; and every tongue that shall rise against thee in judgment thou shalt condemn. This is the heritage of the servants of the Lord, and their righteousness is of me, saith the Lord."*

Another way to avoid dream haters is to be cautious about sharing your dreams. I understand the excitement you feel when God gives you a vision and you know undoubtedly that the vision came from God. I know what it feels like to be so blown away by God as He opens doors and sends resources and divine connections needed in order for you to fulfill your dreams. You are so in awe of God and all that God is doing, you want to share every detail. It feels great to share your story with others, especially when God is being glorified. The dream or vision and the journey to manifestation is part of your testimony. However, if you are not careful - the dream haters will kill your dream as soon as it escapes from your mouth.

I have a lot of associates; people I work with now and in the past, church members, neighbors, pastors, ministers, evangelists, deacons, motivational speakers, life coaches and of course, Facebook friends. Then I have friends; people I've known for some time and who are friends outside of social media sites. I talk to these people on the phone, we go out together and we've visited each other's homes. Then I have my close friends. These are the people within my inner circle. These are the few I speak to on an almost-daily basis or the individuals whom I don't talk with often - but I know I can count on them in times of trouble.

Dream Haters

My dreams are sacred to me and I only share those sacred things with close friends. These are the men and women who will immediately pray for me and the dream God placed in my heart. These friends will support me and my dream in any way possible. They will listen to my ideas and provide constructive feedback. They will entertain text messages early in the morning or late at night. They will pick up the phone and call to encourage me when a text message won't suffice. They will remind me of what God spoke to me when I am feeling discouraged. They will speak life over me and my dreams whenever possible. They will celebrate milestones with me and encourage me to keep pressing. They will push me to go harder and to dig deeper and they will be at the finish line waiting to cheer me across.

As I think about how important my close friends are regarding fulfilling my dreams, I am reminded of my journey to run a full marathon in 2016. For those who do not know, a full marathon is 26.2 miles – that's right, 26.2 miles. When I started running in 2012, my goal was only to run a 5K race - 3.1 miles. I participated in a program called the Couch to 5K program, which was designed to help new runners move from being couch potatoes to runners capable of completing a 5K. I completed the 8-week program and ran my first 5K.

After the 5K, I set a new a goal of running a 10K and I did. Then I wanted to run a 10-miler and I did that as well. Next was a half marathon. I was a bit intimidated by the distance, but I took on the half marathon and nailed it. It wasn't so bad because I was simply adding a few additional miles to each distance as I progressed in my goals. After my 5K, I added 3.1 miles to run my 10K. After my 10K, I added less than 4 more miles to run my 10 miler, then I simply added another 3.1 miles to my 10-miler to run my half marathon.

Progressing from a half marathon to a full marathon was a huge leap. I wasn't simply adding 3 or 4 miles; I was doubling the mileage of my longest run - adding 13.1 miles! I knew this was a goal requiring prayer, mental strength, training, coaching, cheerleading and more. And so, I put my dream out there. I told everyone – not just my close friends, that I was going to run a full marathon. Some thought I was crazy and reminded me that I was 40, it was hot and a whole lot more. But my close friends did exactly what I expected. They embraced my dream and fully supported me from the start.

Then I actually registered for the race I planned to run – the Philadelphia Marathon. My excitement went completely through the roof as it often does when we begin the journey toward our dreams. But then the reality of the work required to fulfill my dreams began to set in. My training started right after the Independence Day holiday, which meant running 3 miles in the scorching heat.

Each time I went out on a training run, my friends cheered me on and celebrated my accomplishment. When my runs got longer in distance, my friends told me that I could do it and I did. When I missed a week of running because I was on vacation, my friends were there to motivate me to get back on schedule when I returned home.

But so far, most of those examples address my better days of training. I was unemployed at the time and able to run whenever I wanted. Plus, it was summer and my children were out of school. In September however, life happened. My oldest daughter was now away in college, but my youngest daughter went back to school. This meant getting ready for school at night, getting her out of the house early in the morning, checking homework, studying and more.

In October - just eight weeks before my race, life happened again. I started a new job. Between school, daylight savings and my new job - I felt like all of my free time had disappeared. Had I reached out to a dream hater during this time of vulnerability, they may have dissuaded me from moving forward. The dream hater would have convinced me that I had no choice but to quit.

My close friends reminded me how much work I had already put in toward my dream. My close friends encouraged me to get my training runs in whenever I could and to not be discouraged if I missed one occasionally. My best friend - my husband, got up in the wee hours of the morning or went out late at night and accompanied me in his car or on his bicycle so that I could safely get in my training run in the dark. My friends were so fully-vested in my dream - they would not let me give up. They kept pushing me and reminding me of my end game. On race day, some friends sent me virtual hugs and well wishes, some cheered me on along the course and some were there to celebrate with me as soon as I crossed the finish line. Those are the types of friends who can handle your dreams with love and care as you move from chasing God to manifesting your dreams.

One final word of advice to help you deal with dream haters; counter their negative, dream-killing words, with positive, dream-affirming words. Words can be used to build or tear down. Proverbs 18:21 says, *"Death and life are in the power of the tongue: and they that love it shall eat the fruit thereof."* In other words, your words have power - creative power, dream- manifesting power. God created the entire universe with the words of His mouth. We can speak those things that are not, as though they were - in accordance with Romans 4:17, *"As it is written, I have made thee a father of many nations, before him whom he believed, even God, who quickeneth the dead, and calleth those things which be not as though they were."*

If you want to avoid the snares set by your enemy, you have to open your mouth and speak your dream. When you give voice to your dream, you are activating the power of your tongue to give life to that dream. Declare that manifestation will happen, then keep pressing until it comes to pass. And remember Numbers 14:28, "*Say unto them, As truly as I live, saith the Lord, as ye have spoken in mine ears, so will I do to you.*" You will have what you say!

Dear God,

I thank you for giving me the discernment to recognize the dream haters in my life and to avoid them at all cost. I thank you for surrounding me with people who will affirm my dreams and celebrate with me as you use me for your glory. Lord, I pray that I will press forward and not be discouraged by the nay-sayers in my life. I pray that you will make my path clear so that I am not tempted to listen to counsel from those who might lead me in a path that is different from the one you have prepared for me. Help me to focus on you and on the dreams that you have placed inside of me. Help me to have bold faith to follow my dreams and to take action as needed to move my dreams forward. I believe that I will manifest every dream you have placed inside of me. It will come to pass in Jesus' name. And for that, I say thank you and I give your name the glory and honor that is due, in Jesus' name. Amen.

CHAPTER 7
Dream Big

As you've probably noticed, the majority of this book focuses on chasing God. You may wonder why it's so important to dedicate this amount of time to chasing God and when we will discuss dream manifestation. Believe me I understand, but we can't put the cart before the horse. We can either await the manifestation of random dreams or we can chase after God - discern His purpose for our lives and allow Him to lead us toward the manifestation of dreams He placed inside of us.

  Whether you realize it or not, you were created to bring God glory. God desires to use you – your gifts, your talents and your life to advance His kingdom agenda. He has a vested interest in the manifestation of dreams He gave you. He wants to be glorified. God puts dreams inside of you and is glorified when those dreams materialize. So at the end of the day, when we talk about chasing God and manifesting dreams – it's really more about God and less about you. If you are chasing God, then you are also chasing the dream placed inside of you. You will see manifestation if you operate in that order. If you attempt to manifest a dream without chasing God, you risk pursuing something which isn't attached to God's will.

  If you don't understand the importance of being a God chaser by now, I encourage you to keep chasing God, even if it doesn't make immediate sense. Keep chasing God and pay attention to how God moves in your life and how He blesses you. If you're currently chasing after God, my prayer is that the preceding chapters helped confirm that you are on the right track toward dream manifestation. If you were not chasing God prior to reading this book, my prayer is two-fold: I pray that you now understand what it means to chase after God and I also pray that God continues to illuminate His Word so that you will chase after Him for the rest of your life.

Finally, it's time to discuss dream manifestation. In the remainder of this book, I will share key steps for making your God-given dreams happen. Are you ready? I am ready and very excited to share this with you. In earlier chapters, we took a few praise breaks because the message was so powerful. Right now, I want you to take a praise break in eager expectation of God speaking to you and your situation throughout the remainder of this book. You should also praise God for those dreams that have not yet manifested in the natural, but are already done in the spirit. Go ahead, this is your time. Just stop right now and say, "Thank you. Lord, I bless your name." "Thank you for manifestation." "Thank you for speaking to me today." "Thank you for the privilege of chasing after you." "Thank you for manifesting the dreams you've given me in Jesus' name."

Doesn't that feel good? As a God chaser, there is nothing like praising and worshipping God. Now we are ready to step into manifestation. The first step in making your dreams happen is actually three-fold. If you are chasing God and want your God-given dream to manifest, I encourage you to do the following: **1)** Dream big **2)** Believe your big dreams can come true and **3)** Write your big dreams down. Let's review those directives individually.

Dream Big

Dream big. You are a God chaser. You serve a mighty big God. You serve a God who is omnipotent, omnipresent and omniscient. You serve a God who is able to do exceeding abundantly above all that you can ask or imagine according to the power in you. If you truly believe this, you should have no problem dreaming big: and get this, no matter how big your dream is, God can do it bigger.

Stop wasting time on little dreams. Dream big. Olympic gold medalist Gabrielle 'Gabby' Douglas is a prime example of a young girl who knew how to dream big. Part of Gabby's big dream was to compete in the Olympics, but that wasn't her entire dream. Having the opportunity to qualify for and compete in the Olympics is a huge dream for many athletes around the world, but that wasn't enough for Gabby: She wanted to bring home a gold medal from the Olympics.

Gabrielle is a young black girl from a single-parent home whose mother knew nothing about how to help her child prepare for the Olympics and also lacked the financial resources required. But guess what? Gabby didn't let that stop her. She held on to her big dreams. But God. Remember God is able to do exceeding abundantly above all you can ask or imagine. So not only did Gabby go to the Olympics; not only did she win a gold medal - Gabby also made history. Look at God. Dream big.

Believe that your big dreams will come true. This is why Gabby Douglas was able to progress from simply dreaming to manifesting her dreams. I encourage you to be just like Gabby. Believe in yourself. Believe in your dreams. Believe they will come true. No matter what your situation looks like right now; no matter where you've been in the past or where you are currently. It doesn't matter where you live or how much money is in your back account.

All that matters is that you are chasing after God. None of those other things can stop a God chaser who has made up his or her mind to believe in their God-given dreams.

Gabby is not the only who had big dreams. Does anyone know Oprah Winfrey? Despite being molested and experiencing the death of her only child, Oprah was able to dream - and dream big. When she was fired from one of her first positions in television and told she wasn't suitable for the industry, Oprah believed in herself and her dreams - not the negativity. As she believed in her dreams, guess what happened? Have you heard of the Oprah Winfrey Show? Ever watched Queen Sugar? What do you know about the OWN network? Oprah was a dreamer and definitely knew how to dream big.

Steve Harvey is another big dreamer. He has admitted to traveling the country doing stand-up comedy while being homeless - literally living out of his car during those times. While he lived out of that car, he was dreaming and believing his dreams would come true. While traveling doing small gigs, he was dreaming of his big break. He was dreaming big. Do you see where I am going? Think about Steve Harvey and his big dreams for a moment - then consider where he is right now. Here are only a few of Steve Harvey's radio, television, movie and print projects: The Steve Harvey Show, Family Feud, Act Like a Lady, Think Like a Man and Little Big Shots. Need I say more? Dream big and believe that your big dreams can come true.

Let's just pause for a moment before we move on to the importance of writing your big dreams down. Between dreaming and dreaming big, you will face opposition. During this time, you will need to dig deep and truly stand on God's promise, believing with all your heart that your God-given dreams will indeed come true. Believing in your dreams simply means that you believe in the possibility of your dreams. I want to encourage you to believe that your dreams are coming true in Jesus' name. Everything (good and bad) that you face is part of the path to your dream manifestation. Remember the Word tells us in Romans 8:28 that *"All things work together for good, for them that love the Lord and are the called according to his purpose."*

Please understand that other people will attempt to dissuade you from pursuing your dreams. Remember that if you are chasing after God, then your purpose surrounds your God-given dreams. People will say that your dream is impossible – but with God, all things are possible. People will say you don't have enough talent, intelligence, beauty, style, grace, education, money or whatever lie they create - but the devil is a liar! You have enough, because you are enough. Believe firmly that your dreams will come to pass and leave the details to God who gave you the dream in the first place. As you chase after God and obey His direction, He will orchestrate 'the how' and will bring that dream to pass in Jesus' name.

Back to the last part of step one: Write your dreams down. God often gives us a vision and we're super-charged, ready to go - but then time passes without manifestation and we lose the fire. A couple of setbacks occur and we lose our excitement. A few challenges arise and we question the dream pursuit and its worth. The good news is that these situations and our responses are common. The bad news is that if you don't recognize the distractions, these common occurrences will murder your dreams.

Writing down dreams God gives can help you overcome common dream killers such as fear, doubt, lack of clarity and discouragement. If you write it down, then you have a written record of the dream God placed on your heart. Trust me, this is much better than relying on your memory. Writing down your dreams allows you the opportunity to review your written record and read what God spoke to you, especially during times of difficulty. When you are discouraged, you can go back to the dream you wrote down. As you read your God-given dream, your excitement will return. As you read your God-given dream, the fire will be rekindled. As you read your God-given dream, you will recall why you are working hard and be encouraged to press through the challenges.

Dear Lord,

*I thank you for showing me what it means to be a God chaser. Your Word says in Psalm 41:1- "**As the hart panteth after the water brooks, so panteth my soul after thee, O God. My soul thirsteth for God, for the living God: when shall I come and appear before God?**" Lord, help me to be a God chaser. Help me to thirst after you. Help me to desire more of you in every area of my life. I surrender myself to you completely.*

Lord, I thank you for the dreams that you placed inside of me. I thank you for the gifts, the talents, the resources, the divine connections and the favor that you placed on my life. I know I will use them all to fulfill the dreams you have given me. I thank you that as I chase after you, you will move me into a season of manifestation.

I praise you right now for the dreams you have given me. I will continue to chase after you as a I dream and dream big. And when you speak to me Lord, I will write it down. I will record the dreams that you've given me, so that I can be encouraged when challenges arise.

I am so excited about chasing you and manifesting my dreams. Use me for your glory. Use me to be a blessing to the kingdom.

I thank you and praise you in the name of Jesus the Christ. Amen.

CHAPTER 8
Check Your Circle

Now that you've written down your big dreams and really believe they can come true, you are ready for the next step. The next step to manifesting your dreams is evaluating your circle. Take a moment to observe the people with whom you spend the most time. First and foremost, you want to identify the God chasers in your circle. As you chase after God through prayer, fasting, studying the Word of God, worshipping God and serving God - you will want prayers and support from those who do the same. These individuals will hold you down in prayer and intercede on your behalf as the Spirit of God leads them.

In addition to the God Chaser, there are three other types of people you will likely encounter. Each person fits into one of these categories: dream killers (haters), die hard-fans (cheerleaders), or dream catalysts (accelerators). Let's examine how people who fall into these categories impact your quest to chase God and manifest your dreams.

We've spent extensive time discussing dream killers in Chapter 3. However, there are a few additional points I want to make about haters based on Joseph's story and my own experience. First, we know that Joseph's brothers were haters -

and to be honest, they had good reason. Joseph was definitely the favorite child and his father did nothing to hide his unequal affection, but there are people who will seemingly hate you without cause.

The hatred without cause is typically tied to jealousy or intimidation within your personal or professional life. This plays out in your personal life with associates you erroneously labeled as friends. You spend time with these individuals. You talk to them on the phone. You go out together. You may have introduced them to your family. Worst of all, you've shared your dreams with them. While you are entertaining these haters masquerading as friends, they are busy envying everything about you. Although haters may never say it to your face, they are jealous of everything from your outward appearance (hair, clothes, accessories, shoes) to your relationships, education, career, material possessions and more.

In your professional life, haters may appear as coworkers, direct reports, managers or supervisors. These individuals see your talent, skill, expertise and experience and are jealous of you, intimidated by what you bring to the table. This is a common trap for those who are not chasing God. A God chaser will see how God blesses you and will praise God - recognizing that the same God who did it for you, can do it for them as well. A hater will despise you because they don't have what you possess. A God chaser will recognize the favor of God on your life; a hater will loathe it.

When you share your dreams with haters - just like Joseph's brothers, your haters will do whatever is in their power to sabotage your dreams. Why would someone who desires what you have, do so much to kill your dreams? Haters are not only jealous of where you are currently - they are jealous of your future as well. Joseph's brothers could not stand that Joseph was the favorite child and abhorred the thought or slightest possibility that he might rise to a position of power that would have them bowing down to him.

Haters will say you think you are better because of your degrees or career, when they simply resent you because they didn't go to college or trade school or because they are stuck in a dead-end job. Haters will secretly hope your business fails because they did not have the courage to pursue entrepreneurship. Haters will tell you that your dreams are too outlandish because the big dreams they once had never materialized. Haters will mock you for believing in your dreams, because they don't have the courage to dream. Haters will have you considering every "What if" scenario for failure, but not the scenarios involving "what if I succeed?"

Haters are slick. You may not always recognize a hater in your circle, but beware. Haters are all around you. Ask yourself a few questions to figure out if you have a hater on board. Does he/she build me up or tear me down? Does he/she celebrate my accomplishments? Is he/she happy when I succeed? Does he/she encourage me to pursue my dreams or try to dissuade me from dream manifestation? Once you've considered these questions, pray about it and ask God to reveal the heart of this person. When God reveals the hater, take action. Remove the hater from your circle or remove yourself from their circle of hate.

The next category is the die-hard fans or cheerleaders. On initial thought, you might think it's great to have people in this category. Die-hard fans love you no matter what. Their love is unconditional. Whether you are winning or losing, your die-hard fans are there for you. Cheerleaders are no different. Cheerleaders are rooting for you from start to finish. When you are up, they are cheering for you. When you are down, they are cheering for you. Who doesn't need that type of support around - especially when you are dreaming big and manifesting dreams amidst opposition?

Felicia R. Phillips

As you chase after God and manifest your dreams, there will be many times when you feel overwhelmed and confronted with fear, lack of confidence, doubt and so much more. When this occurs, it's great to hear your fans and cheerleaders in your ear telling you things like, "Don't give up", "You got this", "You can do it", "You rock", etc. On several occasions, I was tempted to throw in the towel - but these life-affirming words from my fans and cheerleaders were just enough to push me to keep going.

The problem with die-hard fans and cheerleaders is that sometimes their cheers and unwavering support can actually put you and your dreams at risk. How does that happen? When people are constantly calling your name and cheering you on - no matter how good or bad, it can cause you to become complacent. Instead of constantly pushing yourself to do better and always challenging yourself to improve your knowledge, skills, experience or products - you settle for the bare minimum to excite your fan base. Even if you perform poorly - your die-hard fans and cheerleaders still love you, preventing you from immediately feeling the sting of your poor performance.

Let me pause to share a great real-life example. Have you ever watched the show Family Feud? If you've watched the show, you know it consists of two competing family teams who are charged with guessing the top answers provided by average people who were surveyed on specific questions. Now, I don't know if it's the pressure of being on television answering questions in front of a live studio audience, but I've heard some of the most ridiculous answers in response to the questions. The team member responds and after the host, Steve Harvey pokes fun at their answers - the rest of the team members clap and cheer for the team member. This happens over and over again

Not everyone realizes that you don't have to work as hard to please die-hard fans or cheerleaders. They are going to love us no matter what. Knowing this can cause laziness in the pursuit of God and/or our dreams. A preacher might not spend as much time preparing for a sermon because the congregation will love whatever is said. A workshop facilitator might not spend as much time preparing for a presentation because all of the attendees love him or her so much. A businessperson might not spend as much time preparing a proposal because the client admires him or her. Or perhaps you have a deadline for completing a goal and you miss it: your die-hard fans are still going to support you and your cheerleaders will still root for you. Meanwhile, your dream is being delayed.

The final category or type of person you should have in your circle is the dream catalyst/accelerator. The dream catalyst/accelerator shares some similarities with those in the other two categories. Just like the haters, they see the potential that lies within you. They see your big dreams. However, unlike the hater, the dream catalyst/accelerator is not intimidated by your current situation or your future. On the contrary, he or she is excited about where you are going and committed to helping you get there.

The catalyst is also similar to the cheerleader/die-hard fan in that he or she will support you, root for you and cheer you on. The catalyst sees the dream inside of you and gets excited about manifestation. In fact, the catalyst will push you toward manifestation, which is one way the catalyst differs from the cheerleader. The cheerleader will continue to call your name loudly and sing your praises even when you are stuck. The cheerleader cheers for you even when you are headed towards defeat. It does not matter to the cheerleader. On the other hand, the catalyst will intervene when you are going in the wrong direction. The catalyst will give you a loving, but forceful push when you are stuck. When you are slacking, he or she will motivate you to go harder until your dreams are realized. The catalyst enjoys watching you excel and wants to see you succeed.

A catalyst/dream accelerator is an accountability partner or coach. He or she is committed to pushing you toward your goal, but is not satisfied with you simply moving toward it. The catalyst wants you to achieve the goal and to do it *post haste*. In other words, the catalyst wants to move you toward your dreams as quickly as possible. The catalyst will not listen to your excuses like the hater or the cheerleader. I don't have enough education. I don't have enough money. It's too hard. It's going to take too long. I can't. These are all excuses people have used for not pursuing dreams. Haters love these excuses and feed right into them because they realize these excuses stop you from walking in your destiny.

Die-hard fans and cheerleaders will see them as challenges and will be very understanding when you don't manifest your dreams. The catalyst or dream accelerator will view the excuses as opportunities to dig deep, get creative, take risks, leap out on faith and press through to manifestation.

The catalyst/dream accelerator is just the type of person you want to have in your circle, but may be hard to find. Haters come a dime a dozen and you can always develop a base of cheerleaders and die-hard fans. Those are easy jobs. However, finding someone in your circle to see what God has placed inside of you; to call you on your nonsense when necessary and to push you to manifest, can be a challenge. Some of your cheerleaders may do this and even serve as a catalyst or dream accelerator at some point in your life. However, that role is not sustainable for the average cheerleader/die-hard fan.

The catalyst/accelerator is an accomplished individual with a history of success. Please do not chase after a hater disguised as a friend who impersonates a catalyst/accelerator. He or she will talk a good game, but sooner or later you'll discover that he or she is all talk with nothing to show. No fruit. No history. No success story. Instead of catapulting you to your destiny and accelerating your dreams - he or she will leave you unfulfilled, discouraged and questioning your path forward and the vision God gave you. Ask God to send a catalyst/accelerator to you and pray for discernment when you think you've identified that individual.

The catalyst has dreams of her own, but takes pleasure in helping others fulfill their dreams as well. The catalyst helps you uncover dreams hidden to others or buried so deep that you've forgotten them. The catalyst will recharge your dreams and accelerate manifestation. If you are stuck, the catalyst will help you get unstuck. If you are facing an obstacle, the catalyst challenges you to move beyond the obstacle and reminds you that failure is not an option.

The catalyst helps you figure out what is standing in the way of your dreams, then challenges you to move beyond that obstacle. The catalyst helps you continue moving forward and reveals flaws others may overlook. This doesn't mean that the catalyst won't cheer you on like the die-hard fan. It means that unlike the die-hard fan who goes hard for you even when you're losing - the dream accelerator will speak words of life and encouragement, reminding you that failure is not an option.

As I wrote this book, I did not encounter many haters. This was because I practiced one of the earlier recommendations mentioned. I was very careful with my dream to write a book. I only told a few people in my circle, which left very little room for people to hate on me. I did have several cheerleaders/die-hard fans along the way. They encouraged me when I first started and kept pumping me up throughout the process. I appreciate them for that. They did exactly what was needed. The cheerleaders however, did not always hold me accountable. If I didn't mention my book project, they didn't either. If I had an excuse for why I wasn't finished - they were understanding and did not press the issue.

Now that you know more about the types of people in your inner circle, you have some work to do. You should be very clear on who should be in your circle and who needs to be removed immediately. God chasers have no place for haters. Cheerleaders/die hard fans are necessary. We all need them in our lives. But dream manifestation requires more. The catalyst/dream accelerator is a critical. He or she will help you give birth to your God-given dreams. So, go ahead and check your inner circle and make the proper adjustments.

Dear Lord,

Thank you for the dream that you placed inside of me. Thank you for revealing the hearts of the people within my circle. Remove jealous haters who will attempt to sabotage the dreams you've place inside of me. Send cheerleaders who will support and encourage me to pursue my dreams. Help me to identify the catalyst/dream accelerators who will tap into the gifts and talents you've placed inside of me and give me the forward momentum necessary to press through to dream manifestation. I am a God chaser and I will manifest my God-given dreams. In Jesus' name, Amen.

CHAPTER 9

Take the First Step

As I shared previously, the main difference between a person with a dream and a person who fulfills a dream, is that the latter had the courage to actually pursue the dream. In other words, the person who manifests the dream is the person who takes action. The dreamer who is bold enough to take the first step is the dreamer who will one day manifest the dream. So of course, the next step in chasing God and manifesting your dreams is to simply take the first step.

Take the first step! That's it. It sounds so simple, but is it really? In 2013, I decided to participate in a 3-mile walk in honor of my dear friend Charon Natica Jones, who died from complications of Lupus. I remember walking in that event and thinking, next year I want to run the 5K instead of walking.

What just happened there? With that single thought, I set my intention on running in a race to honor my friend. That was in October. The following July, I saw a Facebook post about a running group hosting an 8-week training program to help women train for 5K races. When I saw the post, I recalled my intention to run in the race to honor my friend Charon and decided I was going to participate in the training program.

I was excited to start training, but was also a little nervous. I ran track briefly in 7th and 8th grades, so it felt like I was starting from scratch, which was perfect because the program was designed for women just like me. It was called the 'Couch to 5K' program and would help me prepare to run a 5K race in just 8 weeks.

At the time, I wasn't running nor exercising at all. This training program would require three days of training. I questioned whether I could commit to three days a week but decided I would find a way to make it work. With a full-time job, a husband and two children (15 and 9), I wondered how I would find time to participate in the training program. Although it was a major sacrifice, I entered the 5 am training program.

For the next eight weeks, I trained for my 5K. I started off with 30-second, run-walk intervals. Eventually, I advanced to running for one to two minutes straight. Once we mastered that length of time, we continued to increase our running time. Before I knew it, I was running for eight minutes straight. And somewhere between the 7th and 8th week, we were running all three miles of the 5K without any walk breaks.

With my race just a few months away, I was so excited to return as a runner instead of a walker. I set my intention to run that race a year prior. Several months later, an opportunity to properly train for the race presented itself. Making the connection between my intention and the opportunity to train, I took advantage of the training program. Now, here I was right at the cusp of fulfilling my dream of running this race in honor of my friend. I registered for the race and waited patiently for race day.

Once race day arrived, I was certainly excited, but also quite nervous. After 8 weeks of getting up at 4 am in the morning to run in the darkness at 5am, I was finally at the point of fulfilling my dream. After running in the sweltering heat and humidity during the summer and in colder temperatures during the fall, it was nearly time for manifestation of my dream. After weeks of being completely exhausted after training, it was almost time to put my months of preparation to task. The starting line was in front of me and it was finally time to just go!

      I remember the feeling I had right before I started that race. I remember the thoughts racing through my mind. I remember seeing the finish line in view and knowing that the only way I would get to the finish line, was to first step over that starting line. Does that make sense? Do you see where I am going with this?

      Chasing God is part of the preparation for manifesting your dreams. We ought to seek the face of God regarding our dreams to ensure they are in fact from God. We ought to spend time reading God's Word and inclining our ears to what God speaks through His Word. We ought to spend time talking to God, but also listening to Him. We ought to pray and fast as the Spirit of God leads us. We ought to sit before God in silence and allow Him to minister to us. But once God speaks and instructs us to move, we have to move in obedience to whatever it is He has spoken.

      There are some races I participate in where I can see the starting line and the finish line at the very same time. I have a clear direction of where I am going to start and where I will end up. Because of my training, I generally have a pretty solid idea of how long it will take to get from the starting line to the finish line.

      There are other races which start in one place, but finish in another. Unfortunately, when I am at the starting line for those races, I cannot see the finish line. Have you ever been in that situation? Has God ever given you a dream that seems out of reach? Has God ever given you a dream that is so big, you cannot see the finish line?

When I was first invited to speak in India, it seemed like a far-off dream. However, I took the first step by faith that God brought this opportunity to me and that I would move forward in His strength. I had no idea how I would get to India. In fact, I didn't even have an income at the time. I left a toxic work environment and was literally chasing God, looking to Him to reveal my next move.

I prayed about it, consulted with my husband, then decided to accept the invitation. Because I am a God chaser, my yes was powerful. I was not simply saying yes to the opportunity to speak in India - I was also saying yes to God. I was saying yes to the dream God placed inside of me. I was saying yes to seeing myself the way God sees me.

My 'yes' was the first step towards my dream of becoming an international empowerment speaker. It was also my first step towards seeing myself through a very different set of lens – through the eyes of God. I began to see myself the way God sees me. God saw me as an international speaker, so I had to see myself as an international speaker as well. I am what God sees.

Taking the first step is critical. It is absolutely impossible to finish something you never start. But what is the worst thing that could happen if you actually start? Let's consider my running example: I could start too quickly and run out of steam before finishing the race. This is not likely because I've trained for the race, so I know the pace to maintain from start to finish.

What else might happen if I start the race? Well, it's possible I won't cross the finish line as fast as I hoped. I've trained and have a particular timeline in mind however, I must remember that at the end of the day, it's about God's timing. If I start the race and don't finish in my timing, I can trust that I finished in God's timing.

When I started this book, I intended to finish in time to release it at an event where I was speaking in June 2017. I did it. I took the first step. I started writing the book and was on track to finish by the deadline I gave myself. But then things happened - life happened. I got off track and didn't finish the book by my deadline. Since you are currently reading this, it should be quite clear that the book did indeed get finished – in God's timing, not my own.

Returning to the race example, other things could happen after taking the first step. The race could be harder than anticipated: sometimes in races the ground is flat or may be full of unexpected hills. Of course, I did practice runs uphill during my training, but nothing compared to the hills I often encounter after starting a race.

The same is true with taking the first step in pursuing your dreams. You are going to plan and prepare for as much as possible - however, you will always confront the unexpected after you start. You could retreat and declare "woe is me." You could whine, pout and ask God why. Or you could remember that you are a God chaser, which means you are entitled to some promises. God will never leave you nor forsake you; so even if the road is difficult after that first step, God is with you. God will strengthen you when you are weak, if you just trust Him. You can do all things through Christ!

Now for the last scenario. What if you start the race and just keep running? You may need to slow down a bit. There are times when I can't maintain my running pace, so I slow down - but I do not stop. I keep running. And as I run, I finally realize that I can do it…that I AM doing it. So, I keep on running. When I get to a rough patch, I remember God is with me, so I ask Him to give me strength to endure and I keep running. As I keep running, I find water stations along the way to help me stay hydrated. As I keep running, I see people along the sidelines cheering me on and telling me I can do it. And as I keep running, I realize that I am halfway through the race and I'm tired, but I keep pushing. I keep running. Pretty soon, I can see the finish line. My reward is in sight. So I keep pushing. I keep pressing. I keep running. And guess what - pretty soon, I will cross that finish line.

Do not let anything prevent you from taking that important first step. Stop being afraid to do what God has called you to do. Stop being afraid of pursuing your God-given dreams. Fear is not of God. We believe by faith, which is the opposite of fear. Fear will cause you to miss your blessing. Fear will cause you to miss out on all that God has for your life. Fear will render you useless in the kingdom of God. Just think about all that God could do for you and through you if you were not afraid to take the first step.

This is your time to go back to school. This is your time to operate within your spiritual gifts. This is your time to start your new business. This is your time to run for elected office. This is your time to launch that ministry.

Fear says you can't do it. Fear says it is not going to happen. Fear says it won't work. Fear says do not believe it. Fear stops you from moving forward in God. But I encourage you to say no to fear in the marvelous, matchless and majestic name of Jesus Christ and take the first step. The time is now to start chasing God and manifesting your dreams.

Take the First Step

Dear Lord,

I thank you for giving me a desire to chase after you and manifest my God-given dreams. Lord, help me to trust you to bring it to pass. I believe you and your Word and I will not give in to fear. I know that as a God chaser, you will equip me to do all that you have called me to do. As a God chaser, you have placed gifts inside of me that will help me to manifest my dreams. As a God chaser, you will be with me every step of the way, ordering my steps, guiding my feet and lighting my path.

Lord, I trust you to finish what you have started in me. It will be so according to your will. Lord, I believe you. If there is any unbelief within me, remove it in Jesus' name. Increase my faith as I place my hopes and dreams in your hands.

I will not miss out on what you have in store for me. I declare that what you have for me is for me and I will receive it in Jesus' name. Now bless me as I take the first step and the step after that and the step after that. Breath on my dreams and bring them to pass. In Jesus' name. Amen.

CHAPTER 10
See Yourself Through God's Eyes

As an African-American woman, I am confronted regularly with other people's perception of who I am. Then of course, I battle with my own perception of who I am. I have others on one side and myself on the other. But as a Christian woman and a God chaser seeking to manifest my God-given dreams, there is another perspective I must consider.

I love a song by six-time, Stellar award-winning, Gospel Artist Bishop Paul Morton, which brings clarity to my point. The song, "I Am What You See," is essentially a prayer asking God to help us believe that we are what He sees. The song reminds me of a third perspective of who I am and is another step which God chasers should take to manifest dreams. You already have an idea of what others see and you know what you see in yourself - but what does God see? Do you BELIEVE God when He tells you what He sees? Help me believe, I am what God sees.

It sounds pretty easy, right? All you have to do is BELIEVE, but believing is based on our faith. When we believe by faith that we are what God sees, we are believing God even though we can't see it with our natural eyes. It's that simple. Certain things can hinder our faith. That is the bad news. The good news is that I can tell you how to overcome those faith snatchers and begin to see yourself the way God sees you. I'll share what worked for me.

First, I want you to stop allowing other people – society, corporate America, the media and even your friends and family, to define how you see yourself. If you are going to believe that you are what God sees, you have to learn quickly that it isn't about anyone else. It is about God. What does God see?

As fallible humans, we are limited by the confines of our natural vision. For that reason, a lot of what we see is irrelevant and flawed. We can look back at the past and we can look at what is right now in the present - but that is it. But God! God can look at us and see where we've been – every mistake, every trial, every mountain and every valley. God sees it. God can look at us and see where we are right now – good or bad. It may be hidden to some or on display for all – but either way, God sees exactly where we are right now. God can also see where we are going and be assured we will arrive because He is charting the course. He is the one who empowers us. He is the one who is keeping us. He is the one who will bring it to pass.

God sees all of you - past, present and future, every time he looks at you. God sees the dream He placed inside of you and also sees it coming to pass. You have to see yourself through God's eyes. God sees you employed at that new job. God sees you leading that new ministry. God sees you starting that new business. God sees you finishing school. While everyone else is still talking about what you used to do or how you used to act – when everyone else is talking about your current marital status or your financial situation, God is smiling down at you and seeing the parent, spouse, entrepreneur, pastor, business owner and educator. Do you see it? Say it aloud and believe it! I am what God sees.

The second thing I want you to do is change your thinking to change your story. As a black woman, I have been confronted with various labels; many are not particularly positive or uplifting, nor do they represent the greatness God placed inside of me. I am not a hoe, gold digger, welfare queen, thot or even an angry black woman. I am not too dark, light, ugly, lazy, uneducated or unqualified. I am not too short, tall, fat, skinny or anything in between. I am what God sees.

We often embrace Satan's lies instead of standing on God's truth. We let other people spew out these evil, hateful lies and we accept them as Gospel truth. We let other people create our life narrative, then we accept it and even begin declaring it with our own mouths. Unfortunately, we often let other people tear us down and we cosign on their actions. We allow their destructive language to tell us who we are and we actually declare it with our own tongues. But enough is enough for the God chaser. If you are going to manifest your dreams, you have to see yourself as God sees you.

Proverbs 23:7 says, *"As a man thinketh, so is he."* God chasers must see themselves as God sees them and think of themselves in the same manner. You have to change your thinking to change your story. Don't fall into the trap of believing societal lies. Wrap your arms around the truth about who you are and the greatness that resides within. You are enough. You are smart enough. You are talented enough. You are gifted enough. You are what God sees!

You must remember the importance of the Word of God as you chase after God and manifest your dreams. To begin seeing yourself as God does, you must immerse yourself in the Word of God and find out what God says about you. How can you believe that you are what God sees, if you don't really know what

He sees in the first place? The Apostle Paul tell us in Romans 10:17 that *"Faith comes by hearing, and hearing by the word of God."* God chasers need the word of God to increase faith. We need faith not only to believe God, but to please God. Hebrews 11:6 tells us that *"…without faith, it is impossible to please God."*

So, my fellow God chasers; if you want to believe that you are what God sees, if you want to please God with your faith, you have to know what God says about you. Psalm 139:14 says you are *"…fearfully and wonderfully made."* 1 Peter 2:9 says *"you are a chosen generation, a royal priesthood a holy nation, a peculiar people."* Galatians 4:7 says you are *"…a joint heir with Christ."* Ephesians 2:10 says *"…you are God's workmanship, created to produce good works."*

Those are just a few things the Bible says about each one of us in the body of Christ. This is how God sees us - no matter what we see currently or what we've seen in the past. When you believe God and what He sees, your past doesn't matter. Dreams are yet possible for God chasers. You can still walk down 'Memory Lane' with a heart of thanksgiving and praise. You are not your past. You are what God sees. When you believe you are what God sees, it doesn't matter what you look like. You can walk on 'Purpose Boulevard' knowing that you may be in this place right now - but this is not the last stop. You are a God chaser and you are what God sees. When you are chasing God and believe you are what God sees, it doesn't matter that you can't see where you're going. You just keep walking by faith and believing. You keep chasing God. God sees your dreams. God placed those dreams inside of you. God will manifest your dreams by faith. You are what God sees.

Here is my testimony. I have been so blessed by God, but I definitely had my share of challenges. Long before I would respond to a call into ministry. Long before I attended seminary. Long before I became an international speaker. Long before I became a published author. How did God see me? God saw me as a loving and virtuous wife and helpmate to my husband. God saw me as a godly mother to my oldest daughter, who is now in her second year at Howard University and my baby girl, who is finishing her last year of middle school. God saw me as a talented and award-winning marketing communications professional with a solid reputation and an amazing portfolio. God saw me as a homeowner. God saw me as the founder of F. R. Phillips Ministries. God saw me as an anointed minister at Vision of Hope Baptist Church in Philadelphia. God saw me traveling the country and the entire world spreading the Gospel message and empowering men and women to live their God-given dreams. I am what God sees.

And guess what? God is not done yet. I am just beginning to see myself the way God sees me - and the best is yet to come. My dreams will manifest because I am a God chaser and I am beginning to see myself through God's eyes. I am what God sees. On the heels of traveling to New Delhi, India to speak at a week-long women's conference; in front of an audience of thousands of female entrepreneurs and business leaders from over 120 countries, I am now preparing to go on several international speaking tours with stops in the Bahamas and Dubai within the next 12 months.

I remember when I was first approached by my friend, Dr. Sarah Langley and invited to speak in India. At first, I declined. I didn't think I had anything to offer. I questioned what empowering story I had to share or what life lesson I had to teach. Then I remembered that I am a God chaser. I sought the Lord's face and began to see myself through God's perspective. I did not see an international empowerment speaker, but God did. So, I stepped out on faith and asked God to help me believe I am what He sees. When

I did that, God began opening doors. At one time, I only saw myself as a minister preaching in local churches in Philadelphia. But God sees me as an international preacher, teacher and empowerment speaker. God sees me traveling domestically and globally, making an impact for the kingdom. And guess what? I am starting to see it as well. I see it and I will declare it with my mouth. I AM what God sees.

I pray that you have been inspired by my story. Repeat the words of this prayer and be encouraged to believe and see yourself the way God sees you. I am what God sees and so are you.

Prayer

Father God in heaven, I come to you in the matchless name of Jesus the Christ, to thank you for who you are and who you created me to be. Help me to start thinking about myself and seeing myself the way that you see me. Help me to abandon any thoughts about myself which do not align with what you see. Draw me closer to you today Lord. Reveal my purpose and my destiny so that I can walk in it from this day forward. Lord, I thank you for where I have been. Lord, I thank you for where I am right now. Lord, I thank you for where you are taking me. I believe beyond a shadow of a doubt that I am what you see. Help me to see it. Help me to walk in it. Help me to embrace it. In the precious name of Jesus, I pray. Amen.

CHAPTER 11
Don't Quit

I remember being a babe in Christ and not completely understanding the idea that God - the creator of heaven and earth, actually spoke to His people. As a teenager, I mocked the idea that the Holy one of Israel actually spoke to His children. I recall asking questions like, what does God's voice sound like? Does He have a deep voice like the actor James Earl Jones? What does it sound like when God speaks to you? This was at the beginning of my God-chasing journey.

As I matured, I began to learn and understand how God does indeed speak to the believer. Even better, I actually began hearing the voice of the Lord speaking to me. When you hear the voice of God speaking to you, it is the most amazing experience ever. The very idea that the omnipotent, omniscient, omnipresent God takes time to speak to you is an incredible feeling. What's even more incredible is what God says when He speaks to you.

When God gives you a vision for your life or plants a dream in your heart, it is one of the most exciting things in the world. When you catch a glimpse of where God is taking you and how He is going to use you, it is mind-blowing. Your faith is increased because you have heard from God.

Your current situation may not even be close to what God has revealed for you in the future, but because God spoke to you, you have enough faith to trust Him to bring it to pass in accordance with His word. Nothing is going to stop you from walking in your destiny. Nothing is going to stop you from allowing God to use you. Nothing is going to stop you from receiving all that God has for you. Nothing is going to hinder or deter your dream.

What happens between the time God gives you the dream and when it actually manifests in your life? For the remainder of this chapter, I want to talk about what happens once the excitement dies down. What happens when your faith begins to waver? What happens when you can no longer see that dream or that vision coming to pass? What do you do? Very simply, you do not quit. If you are a God chaser who is ready to manifest the dreams God placed inside of you - do NOT quit!

Pressing forward at this stage in the game is crucial. In fact, it's so crucial that I'm willing to be vulnerable. I'm willing to share some of my challenges and struggles, hoping it will encourage you to keep pressing. This book is a personal testament to my press. I know a little something about the press. I am not just telling you something I pulled from the top of my head. I'm not telling you something based on what someone told me. I am telling you from experience that if you - as a God chaser, wish to move from dreaming to manifestation, you must keep pressing at all cost.

When the opportunity to write this book first presented itself, I was beyond thrilled. I couldn't believe I was finally in position to do something I had only dreamed about doing previously. I was going to become a published author. For years, I had book ideas in my head. But now, the book ideas were going to transform into a published work. My first book was on its way. I was excited. My family was excited. My inner circle of friends was excited!

Establishing a title for the book was very easy. After all, I am definitely a God chaser and had just spoken to a group of young people about following their dreams. I just combined the two ideas and Chasing God, Manifesting Your Dreams was born. I could not believe I had the title for my new book. I then drafted the outline and began writing chapter one. You couldn't tell me anything. I was on fire. I was writing my first book! And honey, when I worked with my photographer and graphic designer to complete the designs for the front and back cover, I was on cloud nine. I stayed up late at night working on my book. I got up early in the morning and worked on my book. You know that feeling you get when you are pumped up about doing something for God.

In May 2017, I traveled to New Delhi, India to speak at the Women's Economic Forum. The trip came right in the middle of what was supposed to be my book completion deadline. I did not let that stop me. Do you know what I did on that 18-hour flight to India? I pulled out my iPad and continued working on my book. Once I arrived in India - despite jet lag and a 9 ½ hour time difference, I still kept pressing to write my book.

But then the first storm hit. I wrote nearly an entire chapter during my second night in India. It was fresh, new content which wasn't on the outline - but it was flowing like water, so I kept going. When I attempted to finish that chapter, I could not find it. I was devastated. This was such an easy chapter to write and I was extremely pleased with what I wrote, but now it was all gone. I did not lose the entire book, but losing that chapter really hurt. I thought perhaps I was doing too much trying to write the book; network at the conference, prepare for the four presentations I would make during the conference and go sight-seeing, all while adjusting to the major time difference. So, I decided to put the book on the shelf until after my trip.

Once I returned from India, the intent was to finish the book. I can't even begin to tell you what stopped me from finishing. I guess I can sum it up in two words; life happens. I got caught up in additional travel for work, parenting and being a spouse – all great things, but I began losing sight of my dream to write my first book. I scattered pictures of the book cover around my house to encourage me, but the reality is that I allowed life to interfere with my dreams and I lost momentum.

At the same time, I also became overwhelmed with the reality of my parents aging and the responsibility of serving as their caregiver. I had assumed care for them a few months earlier, but still had not adjusted to the role. My father – 70 - has Parkinson's Disease and my mother – 68 - has a host of chronic diseases that require numerous visits to primary care doctors and specialists. In addition, they both suffer from mild memory loss. Furthermore, my father was always the transportation in the house, but was no longer comfortable driving. Therefore, the responsibility of getting my parents around to various appointments or running errands, fell on me and my amazing husband. Again, I was overwhelmed and I was tired. I switched to survival mode, which meant I was still chasing God, but was no longer trying to manifest any dreams. I was just trying to make it on a day-to-day basis.

God did not put us on this earth only to survive. He put us on this earth to fulfill our purpose and bring glory to His name. When He places a dream inside us, He has every intent of bringing it to pass. Yes, life does happen. Yes, we get busy. Yes, we get discouraged. However, we cannot allow any of those things to cause us to lose sight of the vision. We must keep pressing. We must keep pressing even as the newness of the idea fades. We must keep pressing even when the excitement goes away. We must keep pressing because our press will lead to manifestation - and manifestation of our God-given dreams brings glory to God!

It is important to note another distinction between a God chaser who is manifesting a God-given dream and a dream chaser who chases any type of dream. When you are chasing a dream which didn't come from God, giving up is easy. You can easily determine that pursuing that particular dream is too hard, will take too long or perhaps there is no longer an interest. However, when you are chasing God and manifesting a dream from Him, you cannot stop even when you want to quit.

Chasing God means that you are seeking God's face and God's direction for your life. Chasing God means that you are looking to walk in your purpose and allow God to use you to bring glory to His name. Chasing God means that the dreams you have are dreams God placed in your heart. These God-given dreams are connected to your purpose. Therefore, if you abort the dreams, you abort your purpose. What is the purpose of chasing after God if you don't walk in the fullness of who you are in Christ and fulfill the purpose God has given you?

As a God chaser, you will also come to understand that the dreams God places inside of you are much bigger than you. Fulfilling your dreams will bless you, but they will also position you to bless others along the way. Just look back at Joseph and his dream in the book of Genesis. Neither Joseph nor his jealous brothers realized when he had his dream, that Joseph would one day become second in command in all of Egypt. No one knew that Joseph would be in a position to prepare Egypt for the devastation in the land and no one knew that Joseph would be able to provide food for his family in the midst of famine.

Since we're discussing Joseph again, consider the times he must have wanted to quit. God allowed him to dream about his brothers bowing down to him, but he found himself sold into slavery. Do you think he was excited about his dream when Potipher's wife lied on him? What about when he was placed in jail? It did not look like this position of power would ever come to pass. Joseph was probably ready to abandon his dream many times throughout his life. We may feel the same way at times, but we have to keep pressing "...*toward the mark for the prize of the high calling of God in Christ Jesus*" in accordance with Philippians 3:14.

There is another point to be made about chasing God and manifesting your dreams based on Joseph's example. Most of what you've read in this book focuses on individuals who are actively looking for dream manifestation. You have a dream that God gave you and you are looking for it to come to pass. I have referred to Joseph's story often in this book because Joseph also had a dream from God. However, there is nothing in Joseph's story that actually says he was looking to manifest the dream God gave him. Instead, we simply see Joseph chasing God. He did not give in to sexual temptation with Potipher's wife because he was chasing God. He was able to interpret the dreams while in jail and even for the Pharaoh, because he was chasing God.

Hallelujah. It's been a few chapters since we've had a collective praise break. If you are not shouting right now, then you don't get it. Joseph was a God chaser with a dream. While he may not have actively chased after the dream that God gave him, he never stopped chasing after God. As Joseph actively chased after God, God was busy working through Joseph's pain, disappointment, betrayal, abandonment, loneliness and imprisonment to bring the dream to pass. Remember this, God chaser. Romans 8:28 tells us that "...*all things work together for good to them that love God, to them who are the called according to his purpose.*"

Because I did not quit, you are prayerfully being blessed by this book. There were many days when I was discouraged. There were many days when I did not think I would ever finish. There were many days when I just wanted to abandon ship. My workload did not magically disappear. My responsibilities as a mother and a wife did not go away. My role as a caregiver did not lessen. I simply refused to quit. Yes, there were weeks when I did nothing to advance my dreams, but I continued to chase after God and God continued to do a work in, through and for me. And this book is the end result of chasing God and manifesting my dreams.

Prayer

Dear God,

I thank you that I am a God chaser and that I will manifest every dream that you have placed inside of me. I know that it will not always be easy, but I am committed to walking in my purpose and fulfilling my destiny. I thank you for your Word that gives me strength when I am feeling weak. I thank you for your word that encourages me when I am feeling down. I thank you Lord for reminding me that with you, I can do anything. I will not quit because my dream is connected to my purpose and my purpose is tied to my destiny. I will not quit because my dream will bless me, but it will also bless others around me as well. I will not quit, because I want to do that which is pleasing in your sight. I won't quit because you did not create me to quit.

I will do what you have called me to do. I will say what you have called me to say. I will be who you have created me to be. Although I may not see it right now, I trust your vision for my life and believe that I am what you see. And for that I thank you.
In Jesus' name. Amen

Conclusion

I pray that you have enjoyed the start or continuation of this journey. Manifesting your God-given dreams may seem scary at first - but once you begin chasing after God, you will soon realize that you have nothing to fear because God is on your side. Be encouraged! You can *"do all things through Christ"* (Philippians 4:13). When the going gets rough, remember Romans 8:28: *"All things work together for good for them that love the Lord and are the called according to his purpose."*

As this book comes to a close, I want to leave you with seven (God's number of perfection) positive affirmations based on the Word of God which will help you as you continue chasing God and manifesting your dreams. Say them aloud every day, especially when times are hard and always believe God's word is true:

1. I believe the Lord is with me. I will trust God and not fear what people can do to me (Psalm 118:6)

2. I will replace fear with faith, which is pleasing to God (Hebrews 11:6)

3. When pursuing my dreams gets hard, challenging or

difficult, I will walk in the full knowledge that God is present in my life, so I have nothing to fear (Psalm 23:4)

4. I will be strong and courageous no matter what situation I face because God is with me and He will never fail me nor forsake me (Deuteronomy 31:6)

5. I will not be afraid or dismayed because God promised in His word that He will strengthen and help me. (Isaiah 41:10)

6. I will believe the truth of the Word of God and not the lies the enemy spews out to cause me to fear obeying God and pursuing my God-given dreams. (Psalm 33:4)

7. God has given me big dreams that will come to pass because He is able (Ephesians 3:20-21)

May the Lord bless you and keep you and may all of your God-given dreams come true as you faithfully chase after God. In Jesus' name. Amen.

www.ingramcontent.com/pod-product-compliance
Lightning Source LLC
Chambersburg PA
CBHW060626100426
42744CB00008B/1517